Praise for
The Essential Handbook for Buying a Home

"The reading flows very well! Very conversational and comfortable. I'm reading tons of things that never came up in our discussions before buying our first home, too many to list, but it's awesome! They're all in tiny, easy to absorb chunks, very helpful. I can definitely picture doing it all over again with this book and highlighting some of these lines. I hope I remember this when I need it, but at least I can come back to it later."

Glenn Sidney
Web Developer and owner of GlennFu, Inc.

"I love it because it's just like I'm talking with you in the room. You write so friendly and not preachy. Highly informative; I really love it."

Susan Beck
Interior Designer

"For fans of *Star Trek* and other outer space adventures you will recall 'The Borg' empire and Spock 'mind melds.' In both cases the connection between the author of knowledge and the student created instant and easy access to a wealth of important and necessary knowledge. This is also true for this fabulous book written by Karen Rittenhouse. Enjoy your new wealth of knowledge and engage in the fabulous and fun world of buying a home."

Fred Fetterolf
CEO Betteroff Properties

D0967896

"This book is essential reading for anyone looking for primer on how to buy a new home. Karen is the real deal."

David Finkel
Wall Street Journal bestselling author of *The Real Estate Fast Track*

"Real world wisdom from a pro. Everything you need to know in an easy to read, well-organized book. Anyone considering buying a home should use this as a guide from the get go."

Ellen Berry
creative consultant and happily surprised first-time homebuyer through the help of author Karen Rittenhouse and her husband Jim

"This book puts the many different aspects of buying a home into a systematic and organized flow that is easily understood. Karen explains every step so clearly that anyone can pick this book up and walk through the intimidating process of home buying with ease."

Jim Williams
Real Estate Investor, Coach and Trainer

"I heard about Karen's book and I was grateful. When looking for our first house in a new town and state, and being a newlywed whose husband was overseas at the time, I walked off a plane in St. Louis, met a realtor whom my husband's company had contracted, looked at 25 homes in two days, and was in shock. Flying home with no purchase, I was reeling with questions: Who is this person? How can I trust her? Is she showing me properties in the right neighborhoods for our needs? What about crime statistics? What things should I be looking for in a new home (first purchase)? What tools do I need to have to figure out the best house for us? Karen's book would have been THE tool I could rely on back then. Thankfully, it's now available to all the other 'newbies' in the house hunt. Thanks, Karen!"

Carol Caffarel
Writer, Speaker, Home Staging Expert

The Essential Handbook
for Buying a Home

The Essential Handbook

FOR BUYING A HOME

Karen Rittenhouse

Southeastern Investments, LLC
Greensboro, North Carolina

Published by Southeastern Investments, LLC
Greensboro, North Carolina

ISBN 13: 978-0-9837752-4-9
Library of Congress Control Number: 2011938427

Second Southeastern Investments, LLC printing: March 2012

Dedication

To all those seeking a place to call home.

"There's no place like home."

Dorothy Gale
The Wizard of Oz

Contents

Acknowledgements

I'd like to thank my many friends who listened to me agonize and question as I went through this process. Thank you for your help and support throughout the journey of my writing.

Thank you to Kathy Haines, our real estate agent, for reading all the parts about real estate agents and adding her input.

Thank you to Jeff Geary, the Mortgage Lender, for his list of lender requirements and reading the parts about lending.

Thanks to my great friend Arminda Lindsay for proofreading (many times).

And a special thanks to the best editor in the world, Ellen Berry, of Phenom Publishing.

Of course, I want to acknowledge the three men in my life, my boys John and Glenn, and my husband, Jim, for always being my reason.

Introduction

Why Read this Book?

Why should you read this book? Because buying a home should be fun and exciting!

As you read, I'm going to answer some of your basic questions: How do I find a house? How do I know what it's worth? What exactly is a credit score? Should I buy a foreclosure? Where do I find a foreclosure? What is a short sale?

You will discover how easy it is to find properties in your area, determine the value of those properties, understand multiple buying strategies, and be confident that the home you ultimately purchase is a smart decision and was purchased at a fair price.

I've been involved in real estate full time since January 2005. After buying and selling more than 150 homes and coaching others to do the same, I've found that most homebuyers have the same questions and concerns. I help buyers and sellers every month and, in this book, I am going to share some of the most frequently discussed questions and answers for people, just like you, buying a home.

People buy houses every day, but you probably don't. The more informed you are going in, the more confident you will be, the more fun you will have, and the better your chance of making a good deal, maybe even a great deal, on your purchase.

There's truly never been a better time to buy real estate. Enjoy the process!

What's Inside?

For ease of use, this book is divided into sections allowing you to read from beginning to end or to jump around easily to specific topics.

We start with *Section 1: The Decision*. Should you even buy a home? Is it a good time? Is it better to rent?

Then *Section 2: The Process*. We look at how to improve your credit score and what to expect when applying for a mortgage.

Next, *Section 3: Buyer Options* covers choices you may be familiar with but not really understand, like short sales, foreclosures, REOs, and USDA financing.

And last, *Section 4: Buyer Basics* will help you with determining your offer, applying for a loan, understanding inspections and closing costs.

We'll sum it all up with the physical part—the moving process.

Being Able to Talk the Talk

If this is your first time buying a home, you will learn a whole new language. Don't panic! There are only a limited number of terms and you will hear the same ones over and over again. In no time, you'll be comfortable using all the vocabulary necessary for buying a home.

For your convenience, a glossary of frequently used terms appears at the end of this book providing quick and easy reference.

Section One

THE DECISION

Let's begin with your ultimate decision: to buy or not to buy? Throughout this book, I've made the assumption that you've already decided to buy, hence the book title. However, you may not be quite clear yet about whether buying is the right thing to do and, if so, why.

To give you some clarity, I'm going to cover:

- Buying versus renting

- The advantages to owning a home

- Whether or not this a good time to buy

- What you need to know about buying

Chapter 1

TO BUY OR
TO RENT

H ave you decided yet? Is buying a home best for you?
Let's begin by clearing up that first decision, to buy
or to rent.

Cost Considerations

Whether or not you are able to buy a home begins with some
basic questions:

- Do you have a steady, regular income (most often from a
job), and is the job expected to be long term?

- Do you currently have "too much" outstanding debt?

- Can you afford to take on the additional expenses of home
ownership like taxes and property maintenance?

- Do you have money saved for a down payment?

There are many great online calculators that will measure the financial differences you will experience when buying vs. renting. These apps do all the calculating for you: Simply plug in the numbers they require. See for yourself; plug in your real numbers such as income and expenses, and instantly you will see the difference between what you will spend over the years renting versus what you will spend over the same time period owning.

Some of the numbers you use are, at this point, assumptions, but this will give you a very good financial starting point. I have two online calculators listed to get you started.

Time Commitment

As a rental tenant, you don't have to worry about things such as how long you plan to stay in the home because you're more quickly able to move than when you have a mortgage. As a buyer, questions to ask yourself when considering the long-term commitment of home buying include:

1. How long will I be in the home?

2. Am I up for a job transfer?

3. How likely is it that I could be laid off?

4. If I buy, how much home can I afford?

5. What is my tax bracket?

Why these questions?

1–3. To resell your home without losing money, you need to live in a home at least three to five years. The longer you stay, the more appreciation and principle pay down you realize. These are home ownership benefits that will help build your personal wealth, and ensure that you have enough equity to sell at a profit. One of the reasons so many people are unable to sell is they haven't lived in the house long enough for it to appreciate in value. Because of that, selling could actually cost them money.

4. This is greatly determined by things like how much you have saved for a down payment, your credit score (the higher your score, the lower your interest rate and, therefore, your monthly payment) and what other expenses you have—cars, boats, credit cards, student loans, etc. Here is the link to an online calculator that will give you an idea of how much you can afford to spend on a home:

BUY/RENT CALCULATORS

Trulia's website:
http://www.trulia.com/rent_vs_buy/

Ginnie Mae's website:
http://www.tinyurl.com/ginniemae

How Much House Calculator:
http://www.tinyurl.com/paymentyoucanafford

Be aware that the cost of home ownership is about more than just the initial purchase price. In addition to the purchase price of the new home, there will be maintenance costs, insurance costs, property taxes, possibly fees for a homeowners association (HOA). If the new home is larger than where you live currently, your utility and maintenance costs will likely go up.

5. What are your income and your tax bracket? One of the advantages of owning is that owners receive tax breaks for property taxes and tax deductions for mortgage interest. When you buy, most of your monthly payment goes toward interest on your

Be aware that the cost of home ownership is about more than just the initial purchase price.

loan, especially in the early years, and those interest payments are tax deductible. The deduction greatly reduces the net amount you actually pay every month to live in the home.

A home is like any other investment—over time you hope it will appreciate and be worth more when you sell. Historically, residential real estate has proven to be an asset that appreciates over the long term.

> *Historically, residential real estate has proven to be an asset that appreciates over the long term.*

Advantages to Owning

- **It's *Yours!*** There's a tremendous joy in owning your own home. You can do what you want to it: paint your own colors, grill out in the backyard, run around, make noise, hang pictures. It's all yours.

- **Permanence.** You and your family feel permanent, planted, and secure in the fact that you control your own environment. There is no landlord to evict you or sell the property out from under you.

- **Consistent payment.** When you own, you know what your payment will be every month. Yes, it will vary over time with changes in homeowners insurance and property taxes, but it's far more stable than rent (provided you have a fixed interest rate on your mortgage). And, you will pay that constant amount for as long as 30 years. That certainly won't be the case if you rent!

- **Value increase.** Even as your payments stay the same, the value of your home will, over time, go up. We've seen that property values don't always go up, but historically here in the United States, homes appreciate about 5 percent per year. Besides, every monthly payment means you owe less on your home than you did the month before.

▨   **Tax advantage.** Most of what you pay every month during the first twenty-three years of your loan is actually interest. Mortgage interest is deductible on your tax return. You can deduct mortgage interest as well as property taxes from your federal income tax and, in some states, from your state income tax as well. Check with a Certified Public Accountant (CPA) for your state laws. When calculating if it's cheaper to rent than to own, don't forget to figure in the tax savings.

▨   **Equity build-up.** When you have enough equity in your home, you can use this equity to get a home equity line of credit (HELOC) or to take out a home equity loan. With a HELOC, the borrower uses their line of credit very much like a credit card, only when needed. Like a credit card, there is a limit to how much you can use. With a home equity loan, the borrower takes the entire sum in one payment up front.

Borrowing against your equity allows you to spend for things like home improvements or college education. The interest rate on these loans is typically far less than on credit cards because they are more secure. The interest you pay on a HELOC or a home equity loan, depending upon your tax situation, is tax deductible.

Of course, borrowing your equity adds to the amount you owe on the property, so it's best to discipline yourself to use these available funds only for something you really need and that grows in value (like a college education) not for a toy or an additional expense (like a boat). If you don't spend the equity, when you sell your home you can use that equity as a down payment on your next home.

If you don't spend the equity, when you sell your home you can use that equity as a down payment on your next home.

▨   **Tax free profit.** Finally, if you do sell, as long as you've lived in your home for at least two of the last five years, you can exclude up to $250,000 profit for yourself or $500,000 profit for a couple from your capital gains. What does this mean? If you live in your home for two years, sell and make a profit of $250,000, you won't pay tax on that profit. Where else can you make that kind of return on an investment tax-free?

Owning a home can be a huge investment in your future. The first home you purchase, if purchased correctly, should lead to an even nicer second home. Over the long term, owning and paying down a home will provide financial security for your retirement through equity growth. The longer you stay in your home, the less you owe and the more it's worth, making it a great investment.

Is This a Good Time to Buy?

Everyone wants to know! The more important question is, of course, is it a good time for *you*? What are your personal circumstances and finances? But, as a general answer to this question, let's discuss, briefly, what's been happening in the U.S. housing market.

House values can be tracked historically. Typically, values rise and fall in a pretty well-defined seven to nine year cycle up, then seven to nine years down. This cycle has been fairly reliable since records began being kept during the Great Depression. More recently, the real estate market was at a low in 1985 and climbed back up until about 1992.

> *We were then in a housing decline until 1999 when the market turned and prices increased until about 2006.*

We were then in a housing decline until 1999 when the market turned and prices increased until about 2006. At that point, we experienced real estate euphoria where everyone could get a loan. Many people who should never have gotten loans got them.

To entice people who wouldn't be able to afford large house payments, lenders gave borrowers adjustable rate mortgages (ARMs). These loans started with very low interest rates so the buyer could afford the monthly payments, but adjusted to higher rates over time, levels they should have been to begin with. Buyers were told, "When your rates adjust up, simply refinance to new, lower rates or put more money down so you owe less."

Sounded great. However, at the same time interest rates were adjusting up, house prices actually declined, so borrowers did not qualify for these refinances. Borrowers could not afford the adjusted higher monthly payments and began to default on loans in record numbers. The market flooded with foreclosures driving prices down even further and, ultimately, the bubble burst!

So, is the seven-year down cycle 2006 to 2013? We'll see. We may not be at the absolute bottom of this most recent cycle, but we're certainly bouncing at or near the bottom. How long we remain here is uncertain.

Some predict we will not see another significant increase in real estate values in our lifetimes. That does not, however, fit the historical model. Housing prices have always rebounded after a period of decline. Add to that the projected population growth, and it becomes likely we'll see an increased need for newer and additional housing.

> The U.S. population is projected to increase by 49 million between 2010 and 2030.

What About Leasing?

After you've done all your calculations, if you find that you're not quite ready to buy but you don't want to rent, you might consider a lease. I'll cover leasing in the next chapter.

Chapter 2

BUYING A HOME WITH A LEASE OPTION

Sometimes, after doing all the calculations, people find they're not able to qualify for a mortgage. If you find you're not quite ready to buy, but you simply don't want to rent, is there some middle ground? Actually, there is. This chapter will show you how a lease option is a great bridge between renting and owning.

Benefits of a Lease Option

Leasing with an option to buy, or rent-to-own, gives you many of the home ownership benefits. You do not, however, have to qualify up front through a traditional lender. Leasing a home gives you time to save more of a down payment and to increase your credit score before you do get a loan.

Lease Option works very much like a rental, but with some of the benefits of buying.

Similar to renting, the lessee/tenant moves into a property owned by someone else and pays a monthly amount to live there.

The difference with a lease option is that the lessee/tenant is actually working toward owning that home at a future date.

The contracts signed include terms for both the rental agreement and the lease agreement. The additional lease terms spell out conditions for the future purchase of the home such as:

1. The amount of time the lessee has to purchase (typically 12–36 months)

2. The purchase price of the home (which is locked in for the term of the contract)

3. The amount of lease option fee (or "down payment" to move in)

4. Any possible seller financing terms

5. Any other terms or conditions of the lease

The lease option fee actually "buys" the lessee the right to purchase the home at a future date and locks in the purchase price. It is typically required at time of contract signing and part of the lease option fee may be credited toward the purchase price. If the contract is not fulfilled, the lease option fee is forfeited.

The great thing about a lease for the buyer/tenant/lessee is that they know they have a contract toward buying the home they live in. While a lease option is in effect, the home cannot be sold to someone else (which is one of the risks with a rental). This gives the lessee time to save a down payment and work toward improving credit.

A lease option is a great bridge between renting and owning.

The lessee experiences a pride of ownership that a renter does not, while still having the flexibility of a rental. If, at anytime, the buyer/tenant/lessee decides not to purchase the property, he or she can move on and the contract ends.

Many sellers offer lease option as one of their selling methods. Too many homes are on the market for the few qualified buyers, and lease option is one way to create a potential sale.

If you find you can't get a mortgage, don't give up your search. Your alternative may be to lease the home of your dreams.

Chapter 3

THINGS TO CONSIDER BEFORE YOU BUY

Prepare for your new home search by creating your ideal wish list! You won't find the home of your dreams if you don't know what you're looking for.

The Wish List

Think big! Describe your perfect home, the ideal home for you and your family. You can modify your list later to pick out the things you must have, but start by including things you would really love to have as well. They may not be essential, but you won't get if you don't ask. Dare to dream!

I wrote a wish list years ago for everything I would want in my ideal home, even though I had no plans to move. Recently, I found that list and imagine—everything I listed way back then I have in my current home! I hadn't even remembered writing it all down.

1. Consider the wants and needs of the entire family. Your home should fit your lifestyle. Do you want a family room, a fenced yard, a fireplace, a pool?

2. Where do you want to live? Does it need to be near good schools or close to your job? If you and your spouse both work, whose job determines the home location?

3. How big do you want? Will the children share a bedroom or do you want extra space for an office or guests?

4. Do you want to be near shopping, near public transportation, near extended family?

5. Do you want an ocean view, a mountain view, to be near a park or a lake?

6. Which things on your list are a must in order to buy and which are things you'd like but aren't essential? For example, how important to you are a large master bedroom with walk-in closet and attached bath, granite countertops, a backyard deck, high ceilings, or plenty of privacy?

Lenders

Before you begin house shopping, it's important to know what kind of financing will be available to you. Armed with that information, you'll be able to quickly offer on a home you may end up competing with others to buy.

If you need help financing your new home, your credit history, amount of debt, income and current market conditions, will play a role in how many choices you have when it comes to lenders and mortgage rates.

The Federal Housing Administration, FHA, recommends that your monthly mortgage payment be no more than 29 percent of your gross (pre-tax) income. But don't stop there. They also state that your mortgage payment combined with your non-housing expenses should not exceed 41 percent of your income. With the 41 percent rule, if you have too much debt for your income, you will not qualify for a loan.

A large salary will not be enough if you have too much debt.

HOW MUCH CAN I BORROW?

When processing your application, lenders take into consideration many things to determine the maximum loan amount you can afford, including:

- Your income
- Length of time with your current employer
- Debt-to-income ratio (how much debt you have compared with how much pre-tax income you bring in to cover that debt)
- How much cash you have available to put down

The Waiting Game

Today, lenders spend a lot of time reviewing your bank statements, tax returns, and job histories. The average mortgage application starts three times thicker than it did at the start of the last housing boom.

It's not uncommon for a closing to take sixty to ninety days, or more. Everyone's backed up: appraisers, underwriters, loan processors. They've all become stricter or, some would say, more accurate. They have far more accountability now than in recent years and don't want to be caught making a mistake or being the reason a loan defaults.

All this means is that it could take months to get a loan finalized, so don't wait to get started.

Mortgage Loan Types

- *Fixed rate mortgage loans* are the most favored type of loan. These loans have an interest rate that remains constant through the entire life of the loan so your payment is fixed and predictable. Your payment will increase slightly from time to time due to increased property taxes and insurance, but the principle and interest portion of your payment does not change.

- *Adjustable rate mortgages* have a fluctuating interest rate. They typically start out with a lower interest rate and, therefore, a lower monthly payment. Over time, these rates adjust, usually up, and can make your payments higher whether your income allows for an increased payment or not. Adjustable rate mortgages have caused many people to lose their homes to foreclosure, so use great caution if you get one. Plan for the increased payment.

- *Balloon mortgages* require the loan balance to be paid off in a fixed number of years. This type of loan offers a low interest rate but only for a specific time frame. Your loan balance will be due in full in, typically, five, seven, or ten years. You must pay it off at that time or, possibly, refinance. Again, use caution as time passes quickly and these balloons come due sooner than you expect!

Loan to Value

Loan to Value (LTV) is a term you will hear when applying for a loan. Loan to Value is the mortgage amount divided by the appraised value of the property:

Loan to Value = $\dfrac{\text{mortgage amount}}{\text{appraised property value}}$

Each loan has a specific LTV. For example, an LTV of 90 percent on a $100,000 property means you can borrow $90,000 and would be required to put down $10,000. An 80 percent LTV on the same property allows you to borrow $80,000 and your down payment would be $20,000.

LTV expresses how much equity the borrower has in the property. In order to protect themselves against default by the borrower, if the LTV is above 80 percent (if the borrower asks to borrow more than 80 percent of the purchase price), lenders typically require mortgage insurance on the property. This is another expense to you, the borrower. If possible, put down at least 20 percent of your loan amount to avoid the additional cost of purchasing mortgage insurance.

> *If possible, put down at least 20 percent of your loan amount to avoid the additional cost of purchasing mortgage insurance.*

Loan Duration

You can request a loan duration of 15, 20, 25, or 30 years. The longer you stretch out your mortgage payments, the lower your monthly amount, but the more interest you will pay over the life of the loan. Typically, with a shorter loan term, you will receive a lower interest rate and pay your home off more quickly.

Types of Properties

What type of home do you prefer: single family, two story, condominium, townhome, manufactured home?

A single family detached home is the most common family home nationwide. This type of home offers the most space from neighbors and the most privacy. It also comes with the most maintenance and upkeep. Do you want a yard? Do you have the time or resources to keep one up? A single family home may be your best choice if you have children or pets, especially if the home has a fenced yard.

Do you want a one-story home (a ranch) or a two story? A two story will definitely give you better exercise going up and down the steps, but check the noise level before you buy. Have someone, perhaps your children, run around upstairs while you stay downstairs and see how well you hear the footsteps and any squeaking floorboards. Some properties are not well constructed and the noise from upstairs can become quite an annoyance.

A single family detached home is probably the most common family home nationwide.

In two story homes, having the master bedroom on the main level is a popular feature and will be important when you resell. Many buyers want to know that they don't have to use the steps daily and like the idea of the children upstairs and the parents down. It's also nice to have a bedroom on the main in case someone gets sick or injured and the steps become unmanageable.

How about a townhome? You will give up some privacy, but townhomes typically sell for less than a single family home with the same square footage. They can be very similar to a condominium, except that you often purchase the land under a townhome, which probably includes a small patio area. Townhomes may be one story or more, but there are no neighbors above or below, just on the sides of the unit. You won't have to worry about exterior maintenance and many come with amenities like pools and tennis courts, even workout rooms.

In a condominium, you will give up more privacy (condos may have neighbors above or below as well as on the sides of the unit). With a condo, you own from the walls in with no footprint of land. You'll pay less for a condo but they have a much slower appreciation rate than houses, and you're subject to all the rules and regulations that go along with living as an attached community.

Homeowners Associations

With townhomes, condos, and many single-family neighborhoods (especially newer ones) you will be part of a homeowners association. As a member, you pay a share of the overall cost to maintain the buildings and the grounds. The HOA fees for condos cover things such as insuring the buildings, exterior maintenance (including paint, roofs, and gutters), landscaping, water, sewer, and trash pick-up.

In neighborhoods with single family houses, HOA fees are used to maintain shared areas of the subdivision including mowing, signage, and plantings in common areas.

In addition to the monthly HOA dues, you can be assessed at any time for expenses that cost more than the association has in reserves (for example, replacing the roof on the condo or townhome).

Generally, Homeowner Associations are a good thing because their restrictions (such as location and size of fencing, whether or not cars can be parked on the streets, etc.) help maintain property values. The downside is that some of your choices are limited (check things like fencing the front yard or putting up a shed to make sure they're allowed), and you have no control over when the fees are increased or by how much.

Some HOA fees can be unbelievably high. There are areas where we have refused to purchase because of outrageous HOA fees. You must pay these fees when due because, if you get behind in your payments, the HOA can foreclose on your property.

HOMEOWNERS' ASSOCIATION CHECKLIST

Before buying a condo or home with HOA membership, know:

- What the fees are and what they cover
- The HOA rules and restrictions
- How much they have in reserves
- How often they raise the monthly dues
- If there is a cap on the amount dues can be raised annually

Location

When shopping for your home, the most important aspect to consider, and the one that will have the biggest impact on the value and quality of your life, is location. You won't live just in the house, but in the area as well. You can change pretty much anything about your home except the location.

Unlike with a rental, where you can move easily, the location of your purchased home will not be temporary, so it's important to consider:

- Is convenient shopping nearby?

- Is the area quiet? Is it safe?

- Is it reasonable distance to your job and family?

- Will you have good access to major highways?

- How are the schools? Even if you don't have children, good schools will be important when you resell.

- Check to see if the property is in an airport flight path, which would mean noise from airplanes.

- If the home is near a fire department, there maybe some noise but close proximity to a fire station often lowers the cost of homeowners insurance (due to reduced response time in an emergency).

- Always check to see if the property is in a flood zone. If so, it may have water issues and will, absolutely, have an added premium on the homeowners insurance.

- Drive around the property at different times of the day. What is the traffic like in the morning, afternoon and evening? What outdoor activity do you observe? Are people walking and biking? Is there heavy traffic?

- Drive to the home from different directions. You may find something that would keep you from buying or maybe a convenient shopping area you didn't know existed!

You can change pretty much anything about your home except the location.

- Where does the sun hit the house? Especially important if you like to garden. If the backyard is shaded, would you want to plant your vegetable garden in the front? Does the sun shine into your bedroom window first thing in the morning? Does any place in the home get direct sunshine for indoor plants? If these things are important to you, take time to research.

- Is the population of the area you're considering growing or declining?

- Is vacant land nearby that may become an apartment complex (which can add neighborhood traffic), a shopping center (which could add value to your location), or a freeway (which could decrease value due to noise)? Check with your city planning department to find out about proposed development in the area.

- You may not mind the apartment complex across the street but will it affect your ability to resell later?

- Will you have slower appreciation because your location limits the number of interested buyers?

Resale value should always be considered when buying because the average homeowner stays in their home only three to seven years.

Expenses

There will be more costs to your purchase than just the agreed-to contract price.

All of the following expenses are real and need to be provided for through what you have saved, so consider them carefully when deciding how much new home you can afford:

- The move—What will it cost for the moving process itself? That depends largely on how far you are moving and if you do it yourself or hire professionals. Across country costs more than across town.

- Utilities—There are often set-up fees to turn on your phone, gas, electricity, and water as well as fees to set up cable. And, remember, the utilities for a larger home will cost more.

- Repairs—Does the house need renovation or updating? Will you be painting, landscaping, replacing window coverings or carpet? Does the house need appliances?

- Closing Costs—These will be covered in Chapter 18, but for now here is a brief definition. Closing costs are additional fees over and above the price of the house and have to do with the transfer of the property. They include a variety of things like loan origination fees, discount points, appraisal fees, title searches, title insurance, surveys, taxes, deed-recording fees, and credit report charges. These costs are typically paid at closing.

- Property Maintenance—If you're buying a larger home, it's not just the monthly payment that will go up. All the costs associated with the home including insurance, utilities, and repair costs will go up (typically, a roof on a 1,500 square foot home costs more than a roof on a 1,000 square foot home). Be realistic and include maintenance items when figuring what you can afford.

Price Point

To determine the price range of houses you can afford (your purchase price point), start with what you are spending today. Do you have money left over every month? If so, perhaps you can afford a larger mortgage payment but, if not, you may need to lower your monthly housing costs.

Even if a lender determines that you qualify for a larger monthly payment, consider your lifestyle. Do you want to spend more of your income on luxuries and vacations, or do you want to spend more of your money on your house and give up some of your extravagances?

> When shopping for your new home, buy only what you can afford, get a fixed-rate mortgage, and protect your home by making payments on time.

If you're like most people, your home is the most significant investment you'll make, so think long term. You're buying it today but you'll be living in it tomorrow, and you'll be selling it at some point in the future. Make sure your numbers work.

Section Two

THE PROCESS

Chapter 4

YOUR CREDIT

t's never too late work toward good credit. How's yours? I guarantee you'll know a lot more about your credit report and your credit score after reading this chapter. And, a good thing, too! Your credit has a bigger impact on your life than you probably know.

Establishing Good Credit

We start the process here because a poor (low) credit score can end your chances of getting a mortgage even before you get started. Here are some "dos" and "don'ts" you'll need to focus on when preparing to buy a home:

Do pay all bills on time! Not just your monthly lease payment (but always pay that first), but everything: credit cards, car payments, utilities, *everything*. Lenders will require bank statements and will run various background checks and credit checks to determine your ability to repay the loan. Make sure everything they see is good.

Don't buy anything new! When planning to buy a home, don't make large purchases: jewelry, vacations, flat screen TVs. *Absolutely no new cars.* Large ticket items can lower your credit score substantially. They significantly change your debt-to-income ratio, meaning that what you owe becomes too close to what you earn and the banks will see that you can't afford to take on more debt. Keep your debt low to make sure you can afford the new house payments. If you must have a new car this year and can't afford a car plus your mortgage payment, it should go without saying, but put off buying the house for now.

Don't change jobs! Lenders want to see a history of stable employment. The exception may be if you get a better job in the same profession with a salary increase but, if possible, don't make any changes until after you've purchased the home.

Your credit has a bigger impact on your life than you probably know.

Do check your credit score. See if there are any incorrect items listed. If so, write to the credit bureau to have them removed. Find a good credit repair person to learn what things you should do first to most improve your score. Your bank or lender can give you the name of someone reputable.

Why all the warnings? I've seen buyers get their credit score high enough to buy the home they've been wanting only to go out and buy a car first because they have good credit. Guess what? They no longer qualified for the home! Or buyers are qualified for their new home, go out before closing and buy new furniture to put in that new home, and then find they no longer qualify for the home.

Lenders WILL do a final check of your credit the day before or the day of closing to make sure nothing has changed. Once you've been approved for your loan, MAKE SURE NOTHING ON YOUR CREDIT REPORT CHANGES!

If you have questions about anything that might affect your credit score and impact your ability to purchase a home, check with the lender. See what qualifications they require before making any decisions.

What is a Credit Score?

Did you know your credit score can determine whether you get anything from a mortgage to an apartment to a job or even a cell phone? It's important to know what is on your credit report and your credit score.

Credit scores are simply a numeric expression of your creditworthiness. They are used by everyone from lenders to landlords and employers to determine your overall financial responsibility and the likelihood that you will repay your debts.

A Fair Isaac Corporation (FICO) score is the most widely used credit scoring system. FICO is one of the companies that provide the credit score model to financial institutions. Credit scores, on the scale assigned by FICO, range from 300 to 850. Less than one percent of the population has a credit score above 800, so it's very unlikely you will ever have an 800 credit score. However, if your credit score is above 720, you will receive the best rates on anything you apply for.

> Having bad information on your credit report or a low credit score may be costing you literally thousands of dollars every year in higher payments.

The biggest problem you will have with your credit score comes from over-extending your credit. Never use more than 50 percent of your available credit. For example, if your credit limit is $5000, don't use over $2500. Anyone looking at your report needs to see that you are responsible and able to pay off the debt you already have. If you've used too much of your available credit, work now to pay down your debt.

Less than one percent of the population has a credit score above 800, so it's very unlikely you will ever have an 800 credit score

The second most important way to build your credit is to *pay all bills on time.* Always keep cash reserves so if you have an accident or lose your job, you can still make your mortgage and credit card payments. Late payments REALLY hurt your credit score.

Who Looks at Your Credit Score?

Pretty much everyone in business relies on credit scores in some way. These are just a few of the companies checking your score and penalizing or rewarding you because of it:

- **Credit card companies.** Whether or not you're approved for a credit card depends upon your credit score. How much interest you pay on that card depends upon your credit score. Did you know that someone using a credit card from the same company might have a lower interest rate than you?

- **Employers.** They're concerned with what risk they'll assume if they hire you.

- **Insurance companies.** If you're a high risk based on your credit score, you're a high risk for insurance companies and they'll charge you a higher rate.

- **Landlords.** If you apply for a rental property, landlords want to know what risk they take by moving you into one of their properties.

- **Mortgage Companies.** When you apply for a home mortgage, your credit score not only affects whether or not you get a home loan, but what interest rate you pay if you do. A credit score plays a large role in a lender's decision to extend credit and under what terms.

Someone using a credit card from the same company might have a lower interest rate than you.

For example, borrowers with a credit score under 600 will not receive a prime mortgage (which has the best terms and lowest interest rates). Those borrowers will pay a higher rate, which has higher monthly payments, and will pay more for the home over the life of the loan.

The higher your credit score, the less you will pay for many things, including the items listed above.

Monitoring Your Credit

When a negative statement is placed on your report, how long it stays there varies by state. Generally, bankruptcy stays for seven years and liens for five years. On average, negative information stays on your credit report for seven to ten years.

Look at your credit report every six months.

There are three national credit reporting agencies, Equifax, Experian, and TransUnion. If there is an error on your report, you must dispute it with all three. These credit reporting agencies do not control what is on your report, they only report what's told to them by your creditors. If you have a dispute with something on your report, these agencies go back to the person who gave them the information and ask for clarity. They handle the process so you don't have to.

A little known fact is that these are private, not government, agencies. If you have a concern with what's been reported, don't hesitate to contact these agencies and request clarification or correction. They will work to assist you in making sure what's reported is accurate.

Credit reporting agencies do not control what is on your report, they only report what's told to them by your creditors.

One of the places to obtain a free credit report is AnnualCreditReport.com. This site allows you to request one report from Equifax, one from Experian, and one from

> *Many credit report mistakes can be corrected simply by writing to the company reporting the error.*

TransUnion once every twelve months. You can request all three reports at once or you can space them out over the year. AnnualCreditReport.com does not provide free credit *scores* of any kind.

It is possible to purchase a credit score from one or more of the bureaus—Equifax, Experian, or TransUnion— when you request your free credit report or reports. If you wish to submit a fraud alert or correct erroneous information on your report, contact the credit bureaus directly either by mail or online.

So, to begin your process, get a copy of your credit report from all three reporting agencies. Why all three? Different items may be reported to each one. If you check only one report, you could miss mistakes that are posted on another. Next, if you see anything questionable, write, call or go online to file your dispute. It takes about thirty days from the time you file your dispute until you have a response.

Correcting Errors on Your Credit Report

Many credit report mistakes can be corrected simply by writing to the company reporting the error. They provide forms to fill out and fax or mail back to them. Along with the form, they will ask for proof, if any exists, of the error. For example, I once had a department store non-payment show up on my report. I wrote the credit reporting bureau stating that I had never signed any paperwork to open that account nor had I ever signed any charges for that account. They checked for my signature and, when they and the department store found my statement was correct, they removed the mark from my credit report. Start to finish it took about six weeks to resolve.

Want to know what a landlord will see about you?
Check out SimpleScreening.com

If there is something on your report that you would like to explain, you are allowed to add your own comments. For example, if you had late payments due to job loss or illness, you can explain that on your report. Many lenders and creditors are understanding about legitimate problems.

If you discover errors on your report, contact the credit reporting agency. You can initiate an investigation online for all three credit reporting agencies. If you use the online service, be sure to also send a letter, certified mail with return receipt requested, as proof of your communication. The addresses set up to receive disputes should appear on your credit report.

Each agency has a phone number listed for disputes. If you call, keep detailed notes and follow the phone call with a letter. Tell, not only the reporting agencies, but also each creditor, about any mistakes.

Experian
P.O. Box 2104
Allen, TX 75013-2104
Phone 888-397-3742

Equifax
P.O. Box 740241
Atlanta, GA 30374-0241
Phone 800-685-1111

TransUnion
P.O. Box 2000
Chester, PA 19022-2000
Phone 800-916-8800

After you've contacted the agency, they will send a letter to the creditor notifying them that you dispute the information they have reported. The creditor has thirty days to respond and explain why that information was reported. If the creditor finds they have made an error, the mistake will be removed from your report. If the creditor does not respond to the dispute within thirty days, the credit reporting agency is required to remove the disputed entry from your report.

At the end of the thirty days, be sure to follow up with the reporting agency to see that they have removed the item from your report. Remember, it is up to you to make sure your report is correct.

For credit cards, the law defines billing errors as any charge:

> *It is up to you to make sure your report is correct.*

- For something you didn't buy

- For a purchase made by someone not authorized to use your account

- For something that is not properly identified on your bill

- For an amount different from the actual purchase price

- For an amount entered on a date different from the purchase date

- For something you did not accept on delivery

- For something that was not delivered as agreed

Billing errors also include:

- Mathematical errors

- Failure to show a payment or other credit to your account

- Failure to mail the bill to your current address if you told the creditor about an address change at least twenty days before the end of the billing period

- Questionable items or any item for which you need more information

> *The money you save for the rest of your life because of a higher credit score is well worth the time and effort.*

Repeat the process as many times as needed until your report is clear of all errors. During this time, work to pay down debt and increase savings. No more late payments. No more debt increase. All of this takes time, but the money you save for the rest of your life because of a higher credit score is well worth the time and effort.

Start better habits today!

Chapter 5

PRE-QUALIFICATION VERSUS PRE-APPROVAL

No sense wasting time and energy finding the home of your dreams only to be told by lenders that you don't qualify for the loan you need to pay for it! How do you know?

Finding Out How Much You Can Borrow

Before most real estate agents will be willing to work with you, and before most sellers will take your offer seriously, you must be able to show that you have talked with a lender and received either a pre-qualification letter or a pre-approval for a loan.

This is step two, after you've worked on your credit score. Start by considering how much you can comfortably afford based on how you live now, and then talk to lenders to find out how much you qualify to borrow. Your research will tell you the price range you can ultimately shop.

Heads-up, you may be approved for a loan payment that is more than you or your budget can comfortably handle. If so, it would be wise to consider homes costing less than the amount for which you've been pre-approved or pre-qualified.

Pre-Qualification

A pre-qualification amount is an estimate that gives you an idea of what you can afford to purchase. It is not a guaranteed amount that a lender will approve.

Heads-up, you may be approved for a loan payment that is more than you or your budget can comfortably handle.

A pre-qualification is relatively easy to obtain, but not very valuable. It is a quick evaluation of your creditworthiness used to determine the *estimated* amount you can afford to borrow.

To pre-qualify, a loan officer will take some of your information (employment, income, assets, current debt) and make an estimate of the borrowing range you should be able to repay to a lender. The loan officer *will not verify any of it.*

You can do a pre-qualification over the phone and without filling out any paperwork. With most pre-qualifications, you won't be asked for your social security number so there is no credit check.

Pre-Approval

A pre-approval determines whether you qualify for a loan and the maximum amount the lender would be willing to lend.

The process of pre-approval involves a *thorough* look into your income and expenses, a look at your credit report and score, and a *confirmation* of income. You will be asked to submit your social security number.

A pre-approval letter from a lender is not a guarantee that the loan will be provided.

So, with a pre-approval, can you get your loan? Not necessarily. A pre-approved mortgage must still be reviewed once you find a specific property. The specific dollar amount in your pre-approval is not guaranteed.

However, as long as no major income or credit changes occur between the time of pre-approval and the actual purchase of a home, the dollar amount of the pre-approval should be good. As stressed in Chapter 4, once you are approved by a lender, *make sure nothing on your credit report changes!*

When you present an offer with a pre-approval letter, sellers know you have already taken steps to qualify to buy their house. Again, a pre-approval letter from a lender is *not* a guarantee that the loan will be provided, but why start the process without knowing what you can afford?

Letter of Pre-Qualification for Loan Application

December 20, 2011

Borrower: Mr. & Mrs. Smith

Borrower Address: 123 Main Street, Greensboro, NC 27410

Pre-Qualified for purchase of property at the following address:
    789 Dream Street, Greensboro, NC 27410

Pre-Qualification is based on ownership as:
    ☒ 1) Primary Residence   ☐ 2) Investment Property   ☐ 3) Second Home

Dear: Mr. & Mrs. Smith

After review of the financial information provided by you and a review of your current credit report, we feel that you are preliminarily qualified based on the affordability, credit and terms you have requested. All of the above is subject to the standard underwriting guidelines of Benchmark Mortgage and any other underwriting investor or agency involved.

This letter is not a commitment to lend funds, but is for pre-qualification purposes only. A loan decision can only be made after completion of a comprehensive underwriting review of the information contained in the Uniform Residential Loan Application for the appropriate loan program.

_____

Lender

Letter of Conditional Approval of your Loan Application

December 20, 2011

Borrower: Mr. & Mrs. Smith
Borrower **Address:** 123 Main Street, Greensboro, NC 27410

Pre-Approved for purchase of property at the following address:
    789 Dream Street, Greensboro, NC 27410

Pre-Approval on this property is based on ownership as:
    __X__ 1) Primary Residence _____2) Investment Property _____3) Second Home

Dear Mr. & Mrs. Smith

Congratulations! We are delighted to inform you that after review of your financial information and completion of an underwriting analysis, Benchmark Mortgage has conditionally approved your mortgage loan request. Following is a summary of key loan terms to which this approval applies:

This pre-approval is subject to but not limited to the following other conditions being satisfied:
- Acceptable contract of sale on suitable property
- No material changes have occurred in applicant's financial condition, creditworthiness, or purpose for the loan prior to closing.
- All closing conditions of Lender and/or Investor must be satisfied including but not limited to: clear transfer of title, acceptable and adequate title insurance, acceptable hazard insurance, flood certification, any/all inspections according to real estate contract.
- Acceptable review of appraisal of subject property
- Satisfaction of any and all investor closing conditions

This approval letter is subject to your acceptance of the terms, and the conditions stated herein as being fully satisfied prior to closing.

This pre-approval is not a commitment to lend funds, but a conditional approval of your loan application and all the conditions listed above are subject to final underwriting and final investor approval.

If you have any questions regarding the conditions or terms of this approval, please feel free to contact us.

Sincerely,

_____

Lender

Chapter 6

FIVE THINGS THAT CAN HURT YOUR CHANCES OF GETTING A MORTGAGE

ere are five important things to consider before you apply for a mortgage loan. Being prepared ahead of time can keep you from making costly mistakes that delay your home buying process.

Changing Jobs

Lenders want to see steady history of employment. Don't change jobs while your application is in process. An exception might be if the new job is in the same field and at the same or greater pay. If you have the opportunity to take a new job, check with your lender before making your decision.

Credit Report Errors

The key to getting the best mortgage interest rate is good credit. One in four adults have SERIOUS errors on their credit reports. The Fair Credit Reporting Act requires credit-reporting agencies to fix these mistakes, but it's up to you to find the problems and ask for the errors to be corrected. I discussed your credit in Chapter 4.

Closing Credit Card Accounts

Paying down credit card balances will reduce your debt and improve your financial picture. However, reducing your amount of available credit can actually lower your credit score. Because of this, you may want to leave the accounts open, even after you've paid them off. Your lender or credit repair person will be able to tell you whether or not closing accounts is best for your situation.

> *Reducing your amount of available credit can actually lower your credit score.*

Getting Rid of HELOC

If you already own a home and have an existing home equity line of credit, or HELOC, it may be best to keep it. You could eventually need it and won't have to go through the trouble of getting one at that time. As with closing credit cards, ask an advisor before you make any changes.

Getting in over your head

There may be a difference between the maximum mortgage payment for which you can qualify (which can be surprisingly high) and the amount you can comfortably afford. It is your responsibility to know the difference. If you're just getting by with your current rent payment and the lender says you qualify for more, think about it! You may qualify for more, but do you really want to live with higher monthly payments? What are you willing to sacrifice to do so (vacations, shopping, eating out)?

One in four adults have SERIOUS errors on their credit reports.

Chapter 7

THE MORTGAGES

I discuss mortgages in Chapter 3; however, the mortgage is such a vital part of the purchase transaction that I want to cover the subject in a bit more detail here.

First, let me encourage you not to be intimidated about applying for a mortgage. Lenders make their money by lending. They want the process to work for you; they need your business. Let's figure out how to get a loan.

How Mortgages Work

A mortgage is a debt secured by a piece of real estate or a loan obtained to purchase a piece of property. You, the borrower, will be obligated to pay back the debt with a predetermined number of payments. A mortgage is also known as a *lien* against the property.

Two things all mortgages contain are the principal, or amount borrowed, and interest charged on that amount.

When applying for a mortgage, lenders prefer to see steady employment (two or more years) with the same employer or in the same line of work. Most will want to see that you have at least five percent of the down payment available through your own savings, and that you'll have money left after the purchase (preferably enough to make two mortgage payments).

Before approaching any lender about a mortgage, get your financial information in order.

Your Lender Will Want to Know:

Employment and income:

- Where you work

- How much you make

- How long you have been at your job

- If your income is full- or part-time, salary or commission

> *Before approaching any lender about a mortgage, get your financial information in order.*

- If you are self employed, which will open up a different set of questions and income verifications.

Cash reserves and assets:

- How much money you have in the bank

- How much will be left after you pay your down payment and closing costs

Outstanding debts:

- Any recurring debts

- How much you owe on those

Your monthly obligations:

- Credit cards, car loans, other loans or debt
- What percent of your monthly income goes to these debts

Down payment:

- How much money you plan to put down
- Whether this is your own money or a gift

Property type:

- Condominium
- Duplex
- Townhome
- Single-family home

Mortgage Types

The three types of mortgage discussed in Chapter 3 include:

- **Fixed Rate Mortgage**—the most popular type of mortgage
- **Adjustable Rate Mortgage**—a mortgage with a fluctuating interest rate
- **Balloon Mortgage**—which requires the loan balance to be paid off in a fixed number of years

Lending requirements change at lightning speed.

Investigate the different types of mortgages and determine which one works best for you.

Good Faith Estimate

The lower your interest rate, the lower your monthly payment and, additionally, the lower the total price of your home over time.

Within three business days of your completing the application process, the lender is required to give you a Good Faith Estimate. This estimate will describe all fees to be paid by you before closing, fees to be paid by you at closing, and any escrow costs you may incur when purchasing the home. It is important to receive your Good Faith Estimate as early as possible so you know what fees the lender will charge, allowing you to shop around for the best rates and the lowest fees.

Lending requirements change at lightning speed. Check with a lender you know or who has been referred to you and shop around to compare loan costs, interest rates and terms for getting your loan. Check with a mortgage lender, a local bank, credit unions and a national lender to find available options.

Interest Rate

When qualifying for a mortgage, a primary concern is your interest rate.

The lower your interest rate, the lower your monthly payment and, additionally, the lower the total price of your home over time.

For example:

- On a $100,000 30-year mortgage, with a 5 percent interest rate, you will pay $536.82 per month. On the same loan with a 6 percent interest rate, you will pay $599.55 per month.

On a $100,000 30-year mortgage, with a 5 percent interest rate, you will pay a total of $93,255 in interest over the life of your loan. On the same loan with a 6 percent interest rate, you will pay a total of $115,838 in interest.

UNDERSTANDING ESCROW

Monies held by a third party on behalf of lender and borrower are held in *escrow*.

When all agreement conditions are met, the money held in escrow transfers to the appropriate entities. For example, property taxes or mortgage insurance is often held in escrow out of every monthly payment until they are due.

When the tax or mortgage insurance payment is due, those monies are transferred from your escrow account and sent to pay your tax or mortgage insurance.

Most mortgage lenders are not willing to risk that a homeowner will not pay property tax or insurance, so they require these monies to be escrowed.

Discount Points

Some lenders will allow you to "buy down" your interest rate by offering discount points. What this means is, you can actually pay the lender for a lower interest rate. Be aware that you are paying the lender the interest today rather than over time. Paying your interest

Lenders are anxious to sell you a lower interest rate because they get their cash immediately rather than waiting for it over time from your monthly payments.

this way will give you a lower monthly payment but will cost more money out of your pocket up front.

Lenders are anxious to sell you a lower interest rate because they get their cash immediately rather than waiting for it over time from your monthly payments.

The lower the rate you want, the more points you will be charged up front.

To buy a lower interest rate, you will buy discount points. Discount points typically cost one percent of the total amount of the loan. Each point lowers your interest rate by one-eighth to one-quarter of a percent. The lower the rate you want, the more points you will be charged up front.

For example, on a $100,000 loan, each point is $1,000. If your interest rate is 6 percent and each point lowers your interest rate by 0.25 percent, two points will cost $2000 and your interest rate will then be 5.5 percent.

Buying down your interest rate is an advantage only if you plan to stay in the home long enough to make back, from your monthly payments, the cost of prepaying your interest.

Prime Plus Points

Depending upon your credit score and the bank's standard procedures, you may be quoted an interest rate that sounds something like, "prime plus two points." This means that your loan interest rate is 2 percent higher than the prime rate of lending at the time of your loan application. If the prime rate that day is 5 percent, your mortgage rate will be prime plus two points (2 percent), or 7 percent.

Upfront Points

Some banks charge an upfront fee for the loan expressed in points. If your loan was $100,000 and your bank charged three points for the loan, the fee amount would be $3,000.

Prepayment Penalty

Be sure to ask if your lender charges a prepayment penalty. Most no longer do; however, some lenders will assess an additional fee if you pay off your loan early.

Shop Carefully

There is much to pay attention to when shopping for loans. Lenders who charge no closing costs and/or no points typically have higher fees but you pay less up front. It may benefit you to roll some of these fees into your loan if you have less money saved for a down payment.

Some lenders will charge an additional fee if you pay off your loan early.

Again, different lenders have different processes and different fees. Always shop around for the best rates and lowest fees. And remember, the banks make their money by lending; they want to make loans and will negotiate some of these charges to get your business.

Chapter 8

TURNED DOWN FOR A MORTGAGE?

According to the Mortgage Bankers Association, about half of all mortgage applicants are currently being turned down. If this happens to you, you're not alone. Don't give up! Let's figure out what to do next.

Find Out Why

Know the reason for the rejection and fix what's wrong. Your lender has thirty days to let you know in writing why you were rejected.

The three most common reasons mortgage loans are denied:

1. Not enough saved for a down payment

2. Too much debt

3. Poor credit history

These three are all things you can work to improve. Only you can make sure you qualify for a loan. Once you have saved more money, paid down some debt and raised your credit score, apply again.

Possible Problems

Credit. Was your credit the issue? Make sure that the reason for the rejection is valid and not a mistake on your credit report.

About half of all mortgage applicants are currently being turned down.

If you were turned down because of information on your credit report, federal law entitles you to an "adverse action" notice. This notice provides the reason for the negative report on which your lender based its decision. When denied because of credit, you're also entitled to a free credit report.

Size of the Loan. Was the requested loan amount too large? If that's the case, you may need to pay a larger down payment or look for a less expensive home, something more in line with what your debt-to-income ratio will allow.

Interest Rate. Was the requested interest rate denied? Try for a slightly higher rate. To qualify for a better interest rate, give a larger down payment and/or raise your credit score. I discussed how to raise your score in Chapter 4, Your Credit.

Try Another Lender

Not every mortgage company or broker applies the same rules, and perhaps another lender has requirements that are less strict. A small local bank or credit union may be more flexible, especially one where you have a personal relationship. Ask family, friends, and co-workers for referrals.

Credit unions are a great place to obtain a mortgage. Our son and daughter-in-law were turned down for a mortgage because the lender needed a two-year history of my son's self-employment.

He'd only had his company for a year and a half. They applied at a credit union and, due to their high credit scores and good down payment, they received a loan immediately with a very low fixed interest rate.

Try a Government Program

The Government Next Door program through the U.S. Department of Housing and Urban Development (HUD) was set up specifically to assist firefighters, teachers, law enforcement officers, and emergency medical technicians. Go to HUD.gov for additional programs that may work for you.

FHA offers programs with down payments as low as 3.5 percent and, for qualified applicants, rolls closing costs and fees into the loan. There is also help available for seniors 62 and older. Check FHA.gov to see if you qualify for any of their programs.

Only you can make sure you qualify for a loan.

Apply Again Soon

A mortgage rejection should not lower your credit score. And, making multiple mortgage applications within a thirty-day period should not negatively impact your rating. However, if you apply for another loan after more than thirty days, this could lower your score about five points for each additional application.

The rules keep changing. Don't give up. If you want to own a home, do everything you need to do and it will happen.

Section Three

BUYING OPTIONS

There are many ways to buy a home, and in this section we'll discuss some you may have heard about but may not understand: short sales, foreclosures, REOs, and USDA 100 percent financing. You need a basic knowledge of each of these buying options to determine if they are right for you and, if so, to know enough about the process to navigate them successfully.

Chapter 9

SHORT SALE

What is a Short Sale? A short sale is when a mortgage is sold *short* of what is owed. As a result of this type of transaction, the bank takes a loss.

The lender accepts the less-than-full repayment of the mortgage in order to avoid what would result in a larger loss for them if they were to foreclose. Because the lender receives less than the actual loan balance, the seller receives nothing from a short sale.

Contrary to popular belief, a seller does not have to be behind on mortgage payments to request a short sale; they simply have to show that the house cannot be sold for what is owed. The lender agrees to *write off* as much of the mortgage as is needed for the home to be sold at current market value.

When a loan is "shorted" and the lender accepts less than the full amount as a pay off, they will often go after the seller for the unpaid balance by placing a deficiency judgment against the seller. It is possible for the seller to be released by the lender from their obligation to repay the shorted amount, or

A seller does not have to be behind on mortgage payments to request a short sale.

deficiency, but not all lenders will do this. Release from obligation to repay is a negotiating process that should be included when working a short sale.

With a deficiency judgment, the seller must pay the difference between what you, the buyer, pay for the property and what the lender accepted for the short sale. You can understand why, in this situation, the seller would not be anxious to sell a property "short."

How to Buy a Short Sale

There are a lot of moving parts to a short sale; the process changes constantly and different lenders have slightly different processes. This makes successfully navigating a short sale difficult. Either study hard before beginning the process, or I suggest enlisting the services of someone who knows and understands the process already. Whether an attorney, an experienced investor or a National Association of Realtors® Short Sale Specialist, find someone whom you trust who has experience in short sales. This expert will be invaluable in helping you through the confusing, time-consuming process.

> *There are a lot of moving parts to a short sale.*

An agent who specializes in short sales will have a list of available properties for you to view. Or when searching for properties on your own, watch for wording or key phrases in listings that may indicate a short sale such as "all offers must meet seller's bank approval."

Making a Short Sale Offer

First of all, when making an offer on a short sale, you must know if you are really getting a good deal. Many people think short sales are always good deals, but, in fact, if you don't know what you're doing, you could end up paying too much.

Short sales take a very long time (in most cases three to eight months minimum), so if you're in a hurry to move, avoid them. If you make an offer on a short sale and the neighborhood values continue to drop, by the time the bank makes a decision, your offer could be higher than the value of the property. If the property is vacant, it could be vandalized or have mechanical damage such as water leaks. In addition, while waiting on a short sale, you might miss a better deal that comes along.

> *While waiting on a short sale, you might miss a better deal that comes along.*

Additionally, rather than accept your offer, the bank may make a counter offer or reject your offer completely, even after you have waited months for their response. During your wait time, the homeowner may do a loan modification or workout and be able to keep the house after all. My point here: Expect delays. Short sales are not easy or fast.

Search only in price points for which you have pre-qualified. Find a property you want to make an offer on and determine your offer amount. The seller's lender will ultimately decide whether or not your offer is accepted, however, sellers also have the right to reject your offer if they feel it's too low. Remember, they may be responsible for any unpaid balance. Even if the seller accepts your offer, you do not have a deal until the lender accepts it.

Once the seller has accepted your offer, you or your real estate agent will submit your offer to the lender with your earnest money deposit. The lender will want to see that you have been pre-approved for a loan so be sure to submit the pre-approval letter with your offer. Your agent should also submit a list of comparable sales in the area to support the price you are offering on the home. Anything you and your agent can do to speed up the process will be helpful.

Typically, your offer will be submitted to the lender's short sale committee. Its decision can take as long as two to three months. Because it can take so long, make your offer contingent upon the lender responding within a certain time frame after which you are free to cancel the offer.

Most short sales are sold "as is" because both the seller and the lender are losing money. Even though they typically will not fix any problems with the property, you still want to know the true condition of the property, so insist upon an inspection. Paying $350 for an inspection could save you thousands of dollars if you find so many hidden flaws that you decide not to go through with the purchase.

Allow a minimum of sixty to ninety days for the short sale process to unfold. Once the lender accepts your offer, they will want you to close within thirty days, so make sure your finances are in order from the very beginning of your process!

> *Most short sales are sold "as is" because both the seller and the lender are losing money.*

A short sale will show up on the seller's credit report, typically dropping their score seventy-five to 100 points. Damage to the seller's credit is often considered not as bad as a foreclosure; however, many creditors make no distinction.

One of the good things about a short sale for you, the buyer, is that the short sale is dependent upon your making an offer to purchase. If the seller does not receive an offer, he or she will not qualify for a short sale. Even after meeting all other criteria, it is possible that no one will buy the home. The seller needs you.

SHORT SALE REPAIR COSTS

Short sale and foreclosed properties are often left in more of a state of disrepair than homes that have been staged by motivated private sellers, so be prepared for some upfront home repair, cleaning, and landscaping costs.

Chapter 10

FORECLOSURE

Popular belief is that purchasing a foreclosed property means buying at a huge discount below true market value. Not necessarily. Let's clear up any myths and misconceptions you may have as well as discuss the best ways to purchase a foreclosed property.

Foreclosure Basics

Foreclosure, simply speaking, is when a lender takes possession of a mortgaged property because the homeowner failed to make the mortgage payments. It is a termination of the mortgage rights of the homeowner. The homeowner lost it; the lender now owns it.

Many foreclosed properties need so much renovation to bring them back to their full value that, by the time you make all the needed repairs, you have invested as much in the home as fair market value or, in the worst case, more. A property in bad condition may not be a good value at any price.

Some foreclosed properties are listed well below what the

A property in bad condition may not be a good value at any price.

former owners paid years ago. What you need to find out is, why? The reduction could be due to dropping values in surrounding neighborhoods, meaning that the discounted home is actually worth less than it was five years ago.

When considering whether to make an offer on a foreclosure:

- Know its true value in as-is condition, its after-repaired value, and what the repairs will cost.

- Don't make a bid or place an offer until you know the maximum you are willing and able to pay.

- Avoid letting your offer creep up until, before you know it, you're hooked paying more than you initially planned and, even worse, more than the current value of the property. KNOW YOUR NUMBERS going in and stick to them!

Once you have determined your maximum offer amount, don't go over it!

FORECLOSURE VS. REO

Is a foreclosure the same thing as an REO (a bank owned property)? No. When a foreclosed property does not sell at public auction, the lender, usually a bank, *takes title*. Once the lender is on title as the owner, the property becomes Real Estate Owned (REO) by the lender. An REO is a property that the lender has taken from the seller and taken title to because of an unsuccessful foreclosure.

Most Common Ways to Buy a Foreclosure

Two ways to purchase a foreclosure are at auction or directly from a lender. Foreclosure auctions have become widespread. They may be held on the property, at the county courthouse steps, or in a hotel or convention center where many foreclosed properties are auctioned at the same time.

Is buying a foreclosure through auction a good idea? Maybe, but there are many things to be aware of when buying properties through auction or at the courthouse steps.

To begin with, are you able to view the property inside and out before buying? Never buy "blind"—without seeing the inside and without having the home inspected before closing. The property may not be such a great deal, after all. We have researched plenty of "cute" houses that looked very interesting from the outside only to be horrified once we saw the inside. You can't always tell what's going on behind closed doors.

> *Never buy "blind"—without seeing the inside and without having the home inspected before closing.*

With an auction purchase, the property comes "as is." Even when buying this way, have the home inspected prior to purchase. An inspection can provide a good idea of what needed repairs will cost. Figure these costs in as part of your "true" purchase price.

Oftentimes, previewing a home before the sale date is not possible with auctions. When buying a foreclosure at the courthouse steps, for example, the lender is the one foreclosing and is not the legal owner. Because they do not yet legally own the property, they do not have the legal right to allow people into the home to inspect it. Buying without inspection is not for the inexperienced. Unless you have plenty of money for repairs, leave these properties to investors.

Liens on Foreclosed Homes

In addition to considerable repairs, foreclosed homes sold at auction can come with liens attached to the property from former owners. These liens will "follow the property," not the seller, and they become your debt when you close on the property. Examples of liens that may follow the property are: unpaid property taxes, unpaid homeowners dues (HOA fees), mechanics liens, or other loans where the property was used as collateral.

> *A title search is the only way you can be certain you are not taking on debt left by a former owner.*

When buying an REO, a property that the lender has taken back from the owner, most of these liens are cleared before the property is marketed for sale. Caution: some liens, such as IRS tax liens, may continue to follow the property even when being sold by a bank, so be sure to have a title search done by an attorney or title company on any property you plan to purchase. A title search is the only way you can be certain you are not taking on debt left by a former owner. I'll cover REO in more depth in the next chapter, Chapter 11, REO.

How Auctions Work

Typically, the minimum opening bid at courthouse auction equals the outstanding mortgage loan amount, plus the accrued interest, plus any fees associated with the foreclosure sale. Oftentimes, this total makes the opening bid at auction higher than the market value of the property. As always, know the property value before bidding.

In addition to costs associated with the property, auctions come with their own fees. A "buyer's premium," or auction fee can add significantly to the price you end up paying. The buyer's premium is a charge to cover the auctioneer's expenses. This fee may be a dollar amount or a percentage of the purchase price of the property. Check with the auction company ahead of time to learn what your costs to purchase will be.

You will need to bring a cash amount with you to bid at an auction. Typically, you will be asked for certified funds or a cashier's check for the minimum bid amount of the property. Better financing options are generally available when purchasing a bank-owned property the traditional way, rather than at an auction.

You may win the highest bid and still not get the property! Banks don't have to accept the winning bid. Ask ahead of time if there is a minimum bid, even if they won't tell you what it is. An Absolute Auction is one where the highest bid wins and there is no minimum set.

> *You may win the highest bid and still not get the property!*

Be aware that, in some cases, the former owner is still in the property and you will have to evict them. The eviction process can be unpleasant (to put it mildly) and expensive and can drag on for months. Know what you're buying.

Preparing to Make Your Offer

You may have heard that banks are eager to get rid of the foreclosed properties on their books. True, but they're not desperate to give them away. Most banks simply service these bad loans but don't actually own them. The loans are often owned by groups of investors who hold the banks accountable to get as much as they can for these properties to help make up for their losses.

When selling a foreclosure the seller, usually a bank, will ask for your pre-approval letter before accepting any offer. Unless you plan to pay cash, you will need a recent lender pre-approval letter describing how much money you can borrow. Banks are very busy and want to know they're dealing with a qualified buyer.

Be prepared to write a lot of offers for different foreclosed properties before you finally purchase one. The great foreclosure deals go quickly and there is a lot of competition for them by both investors and real estate agents. Investors and agents often work together and many foreclosure specialists work directly with investors who are able to buy quickly and with cash. This means you need to have your financing lined up before you begin your offer process. If you want to compete, you won't have time to shop for a home and find financing later.

LET'S SUMMARIZE FOR SOME CLARITY: BUYING A FORECLOSURE AT AUCTION

1. Minimum opening bid at courthouse auction equals the outstanding mortgage loan amount, plus accrued interest, plus any fees associated with the foreclosure sale.

2. Often, especially when buying at the courthouse steps, the buyer is allowed no inspection.

3. These properties may have liens attached.

4. Fees are added to cover auctioneer's expenses

5. These deals often require more upfront cash to buy than traditional purchases.

6. You may have the highest bid and still not get the property.

7. The former owner may still be in the property and you will have to evict.

Chapter 11

REO

What is an REO? If a foreclosed property does not sell at public auction, the lender takes title and it becomes Real Estate Owned by the lender (REO). To move these properties most efficiently, lenders clear the title (get rid of liens against the property), *maybe* do some cosmetic repairs, and put them back on the market at a discount. Warning: Some liens, such as IRS liens, may still attach to the property, so always have an attorney do a title search before purchase to know what, if any, debt you will take on from former owners.

The reason you hear about so many REOs today is that most of the properties for sale at foreclosure auction are worth less than the total amount owed to the bank. With the minimum opening bid at these auctions including the outstanding loan amount, plus the accrued interest, plus any fees associated with the foreclosure sale, these properties aren't selling because the opening bid is just too high.

> *Most of the properties for sale at foreclosure auction are worth less than the total amount owed to the bank.*

HOW TO FIND AN REO?

REOs are often listed with real estate agents so you can find them on the MLS and associated sites like Listingbook.com. You can also find out about them at your county courthouse, often before they're listed with an agent, meaning you are able to negotiate directly with the bank.

There are many ways to find REOs. Here are some online resources for you to use:

- Realty Trac - tinyurl.com/realtytracreo
- BB&T REO - tinyurl.com/bbt-reos
- CitiBank REO - tinyurl.com/citi-reos
- Bank of America REO - tinyurl.com/bofa-reos
- HSBC REO - tinyurl.com/hsbc-reos
- Foreclosure.com - tinyurl.com/foreclosure-reos
- IndyMac REO - tinyurl.com/indymac-reos
- Chase Mortgage REO - tinyurl.com/chase-reos
- Wells Fargo REO - tinyurl.com/wells-reos
- SunTrust REO - tinyurl.com/suntrust-reos
- Fannie Mae REO - tinyurl.com/fanniemae-reos
- HUD REO - tinyurl.com/hud-reos

How to Buy an REO

Many people believe that buying an REO will mean purchasing a piece of property at a huge discount, and it can. If you find one you'd like to buy, how do you go about purchasing it?

First, when banks price REOs less than comparable properties, they often receive multiple offers. Know the maximum you are willing to offer and stick to that price. Sometimes, you'll only have a short time frame to make an offer before the house is sold.

When making an offer, you want the lender to know you are approved for the amount you need, so make sure you are pre-approved before you make your offer. Lenders are busy and won't take time to negotiate until they know you are able to buy. See Chapter 5, Pre-Qualification vs. Pre-Approval.

As with any other home purchase, research the market comps to find what similar properties in the area have sold for in the last ninety days, as well as how similar properties in the area are currently listed. This is important to help you to know if the subject property is actually priced below market value.

Most REOs are priced "as-is," so determine whether or not it will still be a good value after you spend all the money needed for repairs. Don't expect extras like termite work or warranties from the seller. Be sure to ask for an inspection in your offer and have the home inspected prior to purchase. That way, you'll have a good idea of what it will cost to do the needed repairs. Figure these costs in as part of your "true" purchase price. Depending on the repairs needed, the property may not be such a great deal, after all.

If you find things in the inspection that make the property undesirable, you will be able to back out of your offer or renegotiate your offer price.

Put a short inspection period in your offer (seven to ten days) so the bank doesn't have long to wait before they know if you will proceed to closing. Let them know you will move quickly on your offer. If you find things in the inspection that make the property undesirable, you will be able to back out of your offer or renegotiate your offer price.

Many banks are no longer paying closing costs. Find out ahead of time what you will be expected to pay so you'll know your true costs to buy.

If the listing is a relatively new one, it is possible that the bank will not reduce much from its asking price. You may have greater negotiating power making offers on homes that have been on the market longer than thirty days.

Do what you can to learn that specific lender's requirements before placing your offer. And, as with any home purchase, do your "due diligence." Know, before making your offer, how much you should pay for the property. Be certain to have the home inspected and a title search done so you have the best chance, before you purchase, to find any issues that come with the property.

Why Will Lenders Sell for Less than What Was Owed on a Property?

There are a number of reasons and I'll highlight a few here:

1. Many times there is more than one loan on a house. People take out second mortgages or home equity lines which can account for 20 percent or more of what is owed on a property. If two loans were secured to the same property (which is common these days), and the property is foreclosed, the second lender often does not foreclose and gets totally wiped out in the foreclosure. You are dealing with only the price that was owed on the first loan.

2. If there was mortgage insurance on the property, the lender is already paid by the insurance company for any losses.

3. Lenders do not want to sit on inventory. Banks are in the lending business, not the real estate business. If the lender did not receive its minimum bid at the foreclosure sale, they are likely to lower the price to get rid of it.

4. Real estate laws and foreclosure processes vary from state to state. Lenders do not want to tie up their time, money, and/ or legal resources keeping up with all the state-specific laws.

5. The short sale, foreclosure, and REO processes are time intensive and costly. Banks would rather cut their losses and move on, hopefully replacing the bad loans with good ones.

6. The amount banks have to hold in reserves is in direct relation to the amount of money they have tied up in REO properties. A little known fact is that the lender must put aside eight times the amount of the loan in reserves. For example, if the bank owns a property for $100,000, they cannot lend out $800,000 because of that debt. For this reason, banks are anxious to get foreclosures off their books.

IN SUMMARY, ADVANTAGES OF BUYING AN REO RATHER THAN BUYING AT AUCTION:

1. You are able to make low offers.
2. You are able to inspect.
3. Most, sometimes all, liens have been cleared.
4. Some fees are negotiable.
5. You need less upfront cash and are able to get traditional financing.

Chapter 12

USDA RURAL DEVELOPMENT 100% LOAN

Wouldn't you love 100 percent financing? Some individuals get it. For those qualifying individuals, ZERO down payment is required. These loans are available with the help of government assistance programs through the USDA. Let's see if you qualify.

Government Programs

Section 502 Loan Guarantee Program loans are primarily used to help low-income individuals or households purchase homes in rural areas. Under the guaranteed loan program, a loan guarantee through the Housing and Community Facilities Programs means that, should the individual borrower default on the loan, HCFP will pay the lender for the loan.

Under the terms of the program, an individual or family may borrow up to 100 percent of the appraised value of the home, which eliminates the need for a down payment. Since a common barrier to owning a home for many people is the lack of funds to make a down payment, the availability of the loan guarantees from HCFP makes the reality of home ownership available to a much larger percentage of Americans.

Personal Eligibility Requirements Include:

- A moderate income (115 percent of the area median income. So, if the median income in your area is $35,000, then qualifying income is up to $40,250).

- Acceptable credit history—check and maintain your credit report and ask what credit score is required for the loan.

- U.S. citizenship or qualified resident alien status.

- You must be the owner-occupant (you cannot use this property as an investment).

- You must show an ability to repay the loan.

- USDA lenders calculate your ability to repay by taking the mortgage principle, interest, taxes, and insurance (PITI) divided by your gross monthly income. This total must be equal to, or less than, 29 percent. Your total debt divided by your gross monthly income must be equal to, or less than, 41 percent.

USDA PROGRAM WEBSITE

Most USDA loans and limits are state specific. Go to tinyurl.com/usdahomes to learn more about USDA home loan programs in your area.

On this site, you will also be able to check your income eligibility, check their map to determine whether a property is eligible, and contact the USDA directly.

Property Requirements

Requirements dictate that qualifying homes must be located in rural areas. Apparently, however, the government bases qualifying location on old maps! We have a number of homes located right in the heart of subdivisions that qualify yet do not seem "rural."

Homes that qualify can be new or existing homes in good condition. They can be any size or design. These loans are only for homes to be used as your personal residence. No investment, rental, or vacation homes qualify.

> *These loans are only for homes to be used as your personal residence.*

The Loan

If the appraisal is high enough, the loan amount may include closing costs and escrow fees. When this is the case, you may be able to borrow 100 percent of the money needed to purchase the property. These mortgages are for thirty years, and the rates are fixed at current market interest rates.

Remember, even with 100 percent financing, buying a home costs money. You will still have homeownership costs including maintenance and repairs as well as moving costs when you buy.

Section Four

BUYER BASICS

Chapter 13

APPLYING FOR A MORTGAGE

S o, how do you even begin? I contacted a local loan officer and requested a list of requirements to apply for a mortgage loan. You can do the same.

Filling Out the Application

Your lender's requirements may vary somewhat, but this list will give you a good idea of the information you need to have available when applying for a loan:

Income & Assets:

■ Employer Name

■ Employer Contact Info

■ Employer Phone#

Verification of Income:

■ Pay Stubs for the last thirty days (most current)

- W2s for last two years

If you are Self Employed:

- Complete federal tax returns for last two years
- Letter from CPA

If you have Rental Income:

- Complete Federal Tax Returns for last two years
- Current Rental Agreements

If you collect retirement or Social Security:

- Awards Letter
- Last three bank statements showing deposits

If you receive child support:

- Court order for child support/divorce settlement
- Proof of Receipt for past twelve months (print out from state agency, bank statements, cancelled checks)
- Child(ren)'s birth certificate(s)
- Last two bank statements—all pages (most current) with documentation for any large deposits
- Last 401K Statement—all pages (most current)

If you're receiving money from a friend or family member for your purchase:

- Gift letter, signed
- Copy of gift check

- Verification of withdrawal from donor's account

- Verification of deposit into borrower's account (or attorney escrow)

Credit:

- Explanation of derogatory credit (late payments, credit inquiries, charge-offs, collections, judgments)

Verification of Rent:

- Landlord Name

- Phone:

- Complete bankruptcy papers including discharge papers

- Property information for property you're purchasing

- Copy of purchase contract

- Copy of the *cancelled* earnest money check

- Copy of current mortgage statement(s)

Miscellaneous Information:

- Copy of Social Security card and drivers license (legible)— **USA Patriot Act 10/03**

Homeowners Insurance:

- The Company you will be using

- Agent Name

- Agent Phone #:

When supplying required documentation, submit ALL pages.

Other:

▨   Home Phone #

▨   Other Phone Number

When supplying required documentation, submit ALL pages. If your bank statement is six pages long, turn in all six. At the top of each page it will say page 1 of 6, page 3 of 6, etc. The lender will want to see ALL pages and will not proceed if any pages are missing.

After providing all requested information, the lender will pull your credit report, look for anything additional to determine whether or not you qualify to borrow money and, if you can borrow, how much you can borrow. Finally, if necessary, they can begin working with you to improve your credit score.

Allow for the mortgage application process to take anywhere from one to six weeks.

Your credit report will show outstanding debts, open lines of credit (credit cards, home equity lines, any place you have borrowed money, and how much of what you borrowed is still available to you), any late payments you made, any missing payments, collections, foreclosures, etc. Having your credit pulled early in your home-buying process can save you a lot of time and frustration. This is why we covered Your Credit back in Chapter 4.

Having your credit pulled early in your home-buying process can save you a lot of time and frustration.

Your loan officer will give you valuable assistance at this point by directing you to the best and fastest ways to raise your credit score. Some items may need to be corrected, outstanding debt may need to be paid, new lines of credit may need to be opened or old lines of credit closed. Do not do anything to your credit report unless directed by your loan officer. Paying down old debt, paying off credit cards or closing lines of credit may seem like the thing to do, but these moves can actually lower your credit score.

Calculating Your Mortgage Payment

Your monthly mortgage payment always includes your principal payment amount and the interest on that amount. Some lenders also include your annual property taxes, homeowners insurance, and mortgage insurance (if you are required to pay mortgage insurance). This is referred to as "escrowing" your payments. The advantage here is that these annual charges are spread out equally over your monthly payments. If you do not have escrow, these payments will be billed to you in one large amount each year. If you have not saved for them, this can be an unpleasant bill to receive! I prefer to have my tax and insurance payments escrowed.

The amount of your monthly mortgage payment is determined by a number of things including:

- The size of your loan

- The amount of your down payment

- Your interest rate

- The repayment term of your loan (15, 20, 25, or 30 years)

- How often you make your payments (monthly, every two weeks)

The lender is required to give you a Good Faith Estimate within three business days of completing your application process. This is an estimate of the fees due both before and at closing for a mortgage loan. It is important to receive your Good Faith Estimate so you know the lender fees, and can shop around for the best rates and the lowest fees.

Chapter 14

SHOULD YOU HIRE A REAL ESTATE AGENT?

U sing a real estate agent when purchasing a home is not required. Many buyers approach for sale-by-owners or homes listed with real estate agents and make purchases on their own. When buying without an agent, a real estate attorney or title company handles the paperwork and closing process. They will provide assistance and guidance once you find a willing seller and reach an agreement to purchase.

What Will a Real Estate Agent Do for You?

■ **Suggest Neighborhoods.** Ideally, your agent will ask a lot of questions to find out what you want, your desired location, and the price you can afford. Typically, they ask for your pre-qualification letter before working with you to ensure you can afford the homes you're interested in. Armed with all that information, a good agent will suggest areas and neighborhoods for you to consider.

- **Find Houses.** Your agent should comb through the Multiple Listing Service (MLS) looking for houses that meet your criteria including number of bedrooms and baths. They will prepare a list for you and will contact the listing agents to schedule viewings of any properties that interest you.

- **View Properties with You.** Most agents drive their clients to and from the properties they wish to visit. While there, your agent will point out the good and the bad about the area and the property as you inspect.

- **Provide Market Knowledge.** Your agent will have a lot of information at their fingertips, such as price per square foot of similar homes, average sale prices of homes in the area, average number of days on market before they sold, average price reductions over the past sixty days, and more.

- **Determine Values.** When you find a property you are interested in, your agent will comp it to determine the true market value and help you prepare your offer to the seller.

- **Negotiate.** Once you have made the offer, your agent will assist with handling counter offers and help structure an offer that will be accepted by the seller.

- **Supply Vendors.** Most agents have a list of professionals (attorneys, inspectors, appraisers, and contractors) to call on during the buying process. The agent will work on your behalf to make sure necessary communication is handled between them.

- **Attend Closing.** When your offer has been accepted, there are many more steps before you get to the closing table. A good agent will guide you

Using a real estate agent when purchasing a home is not required.

through the inspections and repairs, get contracts to closing attorneys and title companies, make sure documents are signed and presented as needed, and, typically, be there with you when you sign the completed transaction.

DO YOU NEED AN ATTORNEY TO BUY A HOUSE?

Some states require an attorney; some do not. Whether or not one is required, you may want a lawyer to help protect your interests during the purchase. An attorney can review your contracts and assist with the closing process. If using a real estate agent, they may be able to recommend an attorney. Make sure the attorney you hire is experienced in working with homebuyers.

How to Choose a Real Estate Agent

Agents perform a variety of roles, so if you choose to hire one, know your options. A good agent will start a relationship with you by explaining these differences:

- **Listing Agent.** The Listing Agent is actually the real estate company itself. The individual agent who lists and markets the property is known as the "sub-agent" of the listing agent. In fact, all agents working for the listing real estate company are sub-agents. Agents have added financial incentive to sell any "in-house" properties, which are properties listed by anyone in their company office.

- **Buyer's Agent.** Works on behalf of the buyer. Discloses all details of the transaction to the buyer.

- **Seller's Agent.** Works on behalf of the seller. Discloses all details of the transaction to the seller.

- **Dual Agent.** An agent working with a buyer who wants to purchase a listing held by the agent or the agent's firm. A dual agent must be loyal to both the buyer and the seller.

- **Designated Agent.** Similar to a Dual Agent. The broker-in-charge designates one agent to represent the buyer and one agent to represent the seller.

An agent insulates you from direct negotiations with the seller. Sometimes, this can be frustrating. The agent should be able to comfortably lead you in back and forth negotiations that are about more than just price. Perhaps time frames need to be negotiated; perhaps values of personal property need to be negotiated. What about repairs? There is much more to buying and selling a home than the sales price. An experienced real estate agent knows what to do to lead both parties to a swift and agreeable closing.

Best way to find an agent? Recommendations. Whom do you know and what was their experience with their agent? Interview multiple agents and various real estate companies. Continue the process until you find one who best suits your needs. You will be in a close, personal relationship with this agent for months and you need to make sure you can work with them, communicate openly, and trust them as a professional to lead you through the entire process. You want a hardworking, results-driven agent with whom you have rapport to make the process as easy as possible.

There is much more to buying a home than the sales price.

If you decide to work with an agent, be sure to ask if they are working for you or the seller, and ask them to keep all of your conversations confidential.

Your goal, and that of your agent, should be open, comfortable communication and a swift, successful closing.

Chapter 15

DETERMINING PROPERTY VALUE

You've seen a house you like, but how do you determine what it's really worth? There are two main methods for determining property values: comparable sales and cost per square foot.

Comparable Sales (Comps)

Comparable sales are the most commonly used method to determine property value. By comparing similar characteristics between homes of comparable size, value, age, and location, buyers are better able to determine the true property value of the home they want to purchase.

Four Key Factors When Comping Properties

Many factors come into play when comping properties, but four key factors are location, size (square footage), number of bedrooms and bathrooms, and condition. Many more details are considered by professional appraisers to get a "true" value, but these four factors are easy to use, easy to find, and will give you a good idea of the value of the property you are researching.

1. **Location.** You may have heard that, in real estate, the main three things to consider when buying are location, location, and location! Location is extremely important when comparing properties. Where possible when comping, consider only homes in the same neighborhood or within a one-quarter to one-half mile radius.

   If the location is bad, you can't fix it. Remember, when you buy the house, you won't be moving it to a better spot. No, the neighborhood will not improve in the next few years. No, the mall that may be built will not add value. If it is in a bad spot today, it will be in a bad spot tomorrow. Look for a property in a good location.

   Four key factors are location, size (square footage), number of bedrooms and bathrooms, and condition.

2. **Size.** Appraisers prefer to use homes with no more than 20 percent more or less in square footage than the target property. When comping a property that has 1,000 square feet, look at similar homes that are 800–1,200 square feet. The closer in size, of course, the better. If there is nothing of similar size nearby, use the cost per square foot method (which I'll cover shortly).

3. **Bedrooms and bathrooms.** The number of bedrooms and bathrooms is extremely important. A three-bedroom home with 1,200 square feet might be worth more than a two-bedroom home with 1,300 square feet. It also matters where the bedrooms and bathrooms are located. For example, the main floor is preferred; the basement is not so good. At least one bedroom on the main level is highly desirable.

Three-bedroom homes are generally more valued than two-bedroom homes because more families and even couples want the extra space. Likewise, having two bathrooms is a big plus over one bathroom. Heads up: An older three-bedroom brick one story may not be comparable with a new, three-bedroom two story, even if they are on the same street.

4. **Condition.** Even if the numbers are good before you go into the property, be prepared! You may be surprised by what you find upon inspection. When looking, consider the following: Are the appliances new? How old are the roof, carpet, and paint? How well are the other homes in the neighborhood maintained?

Online Sources for Comparing Properties

There are many free online sites, and some are better than others. Search to find the ones you prefer. A good way to check the accuracy of a site's information is to compare its values on homes you know—like your own home and homes of your neighbors or family.

- Cyberhomes.com is a great, quick resource. Click on their Home Values tab. What shows for each property is a price range estimate for that property, the neighborhood value range, and the neighborhood average price. Great information to have.

- Zillow.com is a popular site for property information and gives a similar virtual street map for surrounding property values.

- RealEstateABC.com gives a fantastic chart of recent area sales.

- Realestate.com works for look up of properties listed by real estate agents.

■ Trulia.com is another popular site for property information, stats and trends.

The most useful online source for information about comparable properties is the local Multiple Listing Service, the MLS. This database shows agents many things including the number of days a house has been on the market, whether the property has been updated, whether a seller offered concessions on their sale, and more.

Cost Per Square Foot

Cost per square foot is the second most commonly used method to determine property value. It will help you compare properties that have a number of differences or for properties being sold at different prices.

To calculate the cost per square foot, divide the sale price of the house by the number of square feet:

Price / Square Feet

You may notice that the cost per square foot on a one story is higher than on a two story with the same square footage.

Example: If the house asking price is $100,000 and has 1,200 square feet, divide $100,000 by 1,200. The answer is the cost of that house per square foot—$83.33. Use your current residence for practice. Take the market value of your home and divide that number by the number of square feet in your home. How much is your home per square foot?

You may notice that the cost per square foot on a one story is higher than on a two story with the same square footage. The reason is that a two-story home can have the same square footage on a much smaller lot. The difference in price is the difference in land value.

Additional Factors to Consider

There are other factors to consider that affect the value of a home, but generally these are less important than location, size, and number of bedrooms and bathrooms. Some of these will be more difficult unless you have an agent. When looking through local comps, there are a number of additional things you, or they, need to compare:

1. **Distance.** Use comps located within a quarter-mile radius of the subject property. If you are in an area with little market activity or in a rural area, using comparable properties from farther away may be necessary.

2. **Date of Sale of Comp.** Use recent home sales (ones that have taken place within the last six months). If the market is slow, you may need to go back twelve months.

3. **Construction.** If the subject is an all brick house, use comps that are all brick; if it is a wood or vinyl-sided house, use comps that have wood or vinyl siding.

4. **Condition.** Even when everything else is the same, obviously, a house in poor condition will have a lower value than one that has been kept up.

5. **Age.** Where possible, use comps that are the same age as your property. Try to stay within three years difference, either older or younger. Keep in mind that a rehabbed property does not hold the same value as a new one.

Square footage is determined by the amount of heated square feet.

6. **Square Footage.** Square footage is determined by the amount of heated square feet. Unheated basements and garages do not count in square footage. Try to keep your comps within 100 square feet.

7. **Number of floors.** Use properties that have the same number as your subject property.

8. **Basement.** If the subject is on a crawl space or slab, use comps on crawl spaces and slabs. If the subject has a basement, pull comps with basements. Try to keep the square footage of the basements as close as possible.

   The value of some housing features varies depending upon the region of the country. Basements often come with homes in the North where the freeze line is deep so the foundations, or basements, are also. In warmer climates the freeze line, if there is any, is very shallow so all that is required for the foundation is a crawl space under the house. Some Southern homes are built directly on top of concrete slabs and have no crawl space.

9. **Garage or Carport.** Again, use same for same.

10. **Lot Size.** Compare similar size lots.

11. **How long has the property been on the market?** A long time on the market may indicate that it's overpriced. This can indicate a very eager seller or, on the other hand, a seller who is not willing to reduce the asking price!

12. **Why are they selling?** Sometimes you can find out. If the seller has been transferred and is moving soon, he or she is most likely motivated. If a seller is not willing to move without a high enough offer, he or she is not so motivated.

Basements often come with homes in the North where the freeze line is deep so the foundations, or basements, are also.

You get the idea. The more similarities between properties, the easier it will be to comp the property you wish to purchase. It is often very difficult to find like-kind comparisons. When your comps vary significantly from your subject property, they are not really comps! You'll need to adjust your numbers accordingly and this takes some experience and training. If it were easy, we wouldn't need appraisers!

In Summary

Property "fair market value" is determined by looking at and comparing recent sale prices of similar properties in the area. When determining value, it's best to compare prices of properties that have sold rather than using properties that are still listed for sale, as most homes sell for less than the listed price.

A great way to begin learning value is to search real estate listings and visit open houses in the areas you prefer. This will help you get a feel for the local pricing. When visiting open houses, go to ones that are more expensive and less expensive than your target price. The more you see, the more you will begin to understand what a property is worth and what value things like a bedroom or bathroom add.

Property "fair market value" is determined by looking at and comparing recent sale prices of similar properties in the area.

Use online resources. There is a lot of property information available with the click of a mouse. Find everything you need to know before you make your offer!

Chapter 16

MAKING AN OFFER

Once you've arrived at this point, you've found a house you'd like to call home. How exciting! New questions: What's too much? What's too little? What's just right? Let's break down the different aspects of making your offer.

What's the Right Amount?

In a depressed real estate market, no seller really expects a full price offer. During the past ten years, offers nationally averaged 3 percent to 5 percent below asking price. Experts say the average national discount below the asking price today is about 7 percent. Sellers are not surprised when you offer less than they're asking.

Before you meet with the seller, make sure you've already done your homework and determined (1) that you want the property, (2) its market value, and (3) what you are willing to pay for it. Use the information you gained when comping the property (discussed in Chapter 15) to help both you and the seller come to an agreement about what the home is worth.

Determine what you can afford by adding your new mortgage payment plus all additional costs that will occur with the purchase, including inspections, taxes, repairs and updates you plan to do when you move in, utility increases above what you are currently paying, and yard maintenance. It's easy to fall in love with the idea of a particular house and offer more than you can comfortably live with. This list helps you recognize there are more costs to buying than just the purchase price itself.

Experts say the average national discount below the asking price today is about 7 percent.

When asking the seller to discount the listing price, defend your offer by pointing out your costs for inspections, taxes, repairs, and updates needed on the home. The seller may be willing to pick up some of these costs for you by agreeing to lower their asking price.

Everything's Negotiable!

Did you see something in the house that you want the sellers to leave? Ask for these items in your offer. Items that are often part of the negotiation include appliances, window treatments, light fixtures, furnishings, yard equipment such as lawn mowers, sheds, washers/dryers, fences (yes, we had a seller take one when he left so write it down), plants and pots on the deck. What did you see that made you love the home?

To make the purchase of their home attractive to buyers, sellers are currently paying most of the closing costs. It's a buyer's market, so sellers are taking larger discounts and picking up more of the back end (closing) costs than in past years. You should absolutely request this in your offer.

When negotiating, investors often make very low offers. For them, of course, it does not matter if they end up purchasing the property; they aren't emotionally attached and will move onto the next. You, however, if you love it, should make a reasonable offer. Don't offer so low that you offend the seller. However, once you have made an offer, you can't go back and lower it, so don't start too high!

How Much Is Real Estate Commission?

The norm in most states is 6 percent real estate commission: 3 percent to the listing agent and 3 percent to the selling agent. Check your area—the amount can vary depending not just on state but on location such as mountain or waterfront properties as well.

The seller knows commission will be a cost when they list their property. They expect to pay it to their listing agent as well as to any real estate agent who brings them a buyer. If you buy from a for-sale-by-owner, you can negotiate the cost of commission to reduce your offer price since, if you buy their home without an agent, they won't be paying commission.

Sellers are taking larger discounts and picking up more of the back end (closing) costs than in past years.

How Much Earnest Money Should You Put Down?

Earnest money is a deposit that you give when you place your offer. It shows the seller that you are serious about purchasing their home. Typically, earnest money is 1 percent to 5 percent of the price you're offering. The less you put down, the less you risk losing if you back out of the deal. The more you put down, the more serious the seller considers your offer.

Your agent can help you determine the amount to submit with your offer. If your offer is accepted, the earnest money becomes part of your down payment. If your offer is rejected, the earnest money is returned to you. If you back out of the deal, depending upon the circumstances, you may forfeit your earnest money deposit.

What Is a Home Warranty?

In your offer, request that the seller provide a good home warranty. Cost is typically $350–$500, and the service contract will cover things like the repair or replacement of appliances and heating and air systems if they break down in the first year of homeownership.

What Is an Appliance Allowance?

Are the appliances dated? Rather than replacing them, many sellers give an allowance (for example, $1,000) toward replacement, allowing the buyer to purchase his or her own appliances after closing.

Counter Offers

When you make an offer, the seller is not required to respond. Typically, the offer states a time frame for the seller's response, after which the offer automatically expires. Most often, rather than accepting or rejecting your first offer, the seller instead makes a counter offer.

> *If you make an offer or counter offer and change your mind, you can back out.*

You present an offer to the seller. The seller responds with a counter offer because your offer was, to them, unacceptable. This counter revises the initial offer. Responding with a counter offer is a way to decline a previous offer while continuing negotiations.

Counter offers are a normal part of the buying/selling process. Expect your seller to respond to you with a counter. This is perfectly acceptable because (1) it is common practice and (2) if they accept your first offer, you may have offered too much! The counter offer is where the negotiations really begin and you can start to understand the seller's true wishes.

The seller may counter your offer with a higher price, and/or they may change some of the terms of your offer. They may want a higher down payment, need an earlier closing date, refuse to leave the appliances, etc. Counter offers are considered new offers and the process starts over with each new counter.

You may accept the counter, or you may make adjustments and counter the counter offer, (making yours a second counter offer, or counter offer No. 2). There is no limit to the number of counter offers that can go back and forth. Like with the original offer, no response is required to a counter, so they contain expiration times just like the original purchase offer.

When you receive a counter, it is not an outright rejection of your offer. The seller is continuing the negotiation, which is good! The goal is to keep the counter offers going because, as soon as one of you stops countering without an acceptance, the deal is dead.

Responding with a counter offer is a way to decline a previous offer while continuing negotiations.

Typical response time for an offer or a counter offer is twenty-four hours. If you make an offer or counter offer and change your mind, you can back out. You are allowed to withdraw your offer as long as the seller has not yet accepted it. Once an acceptance is communicated to you or your agent, and/or to the seller or the seller's agent, you have a contract.

You never have to accept a seller counter. If you do not agree with what they are requiring from you as the buyer, walk away. There are plenty of properties for sale and new ones come on the market every day. Any time the seller does not accept your offer, you immediately get your deposit back.

Agents must present, to the seller, any legal offer you make in writing that is accompanied by a deposit check. Your agent can never refuse to present an offer because he or she feels it is too low. If your agent refuses, find another agent.

Always Request an Inspection

Make your offer contingent upon the inspection meaning that, if you do not approve after inspection, the deal is dead and you get your earnest money back. Have the inspection completed as quickly as possible so that both you and the seller know whether you have a completed contract. Two weeks is a good time frame to allow.

If at all possible, attend the inspection. There is no better way to learn about the property than to be there as the inspector goes through and makes comments. You will receive a written copy of the findings. It is your choice to have any or all of the items repaired. Repairs will be negotiated between you and the seller, so work to arrive at something acceptable for both of you. It's a negotiation, after all, and everyone wants to walk away feeling that they "won."

There is no better way to learn about the property than to be there as the inspector goes through and makes comments.

Chapter 17

HOME INSPECTIONS: WHAT TO LOOK FOR

You'll hire, and pay for, a licensed home inspector. You and your family members or friends do not have the trained eye to find the hidden (and, sometimes, not so hidden) flaws or weaknesses of the structure. An inspection is a wonderful thing and your opportunity to learn what to expect after the deal is closed.

Why Do You Need an Inspection?

Always get a home inspection. Chances are, you won't need to request it, because most lenders require an inspection before closing. They want to know the condition of the property they are lending against.

But why do you need an inspection, especially when everything looks okay? Because you don't know what you don't know. A trained eye can find mechanical and hidden problems that you may overlook. Better to spend $250 for an inspection and walk away from what you thought was a "deal" than to save that money and later discover $15,000 in foundation and water issues that you missed on your own.

This actually happened to me. I personally inspected a property and purchased in the heat of summer. (No, I did not pay an inspector to check this property.) When rains returned in the fall, furniture in the newly finished basement literally floated in all the water. $15,000 and three months later, the issue was resolved.

Always get a home inspection.

Even with new construction, do not assume the builder or contractors did everything right simply because the house passed code. Having bought new construction myself, I can assure you there can be as many problems after closing as with older homes.

Getting the Most out of an Inspection

A home inspector will check the mechanical, structural, and electrical condition of the structure. He will look for problems and defects, and make you aware of issues and repairs that need attention. His focus includes: roof, siding, plumbing, electrical systems, heating and air units, ventilation, insulation, water heater, pest infiltration, foundation, doors, ceilings, walls, floor, and your water source and quality.

Be sure to hire someone who is competent, thorough, and trustworthy. Get dependable referrals and do some research before choosing an inspector. Ask about licensing, professional affiliations and credentials, and whether the inspector carries errors and omissions insurance (to cover problems missed that you may be stuck with later).

When having a property inspected, go along with the inspector, ask questions and listen to their professional opinion about the house. Reading a written report is not nearly as valuable as being there, discussing items as they are found, and leaving with a truer picture of the condition of the property.

HOME INSPECTION CHECKLIST

For a full list of what your home inspection should cover, go online and check out the American Home Inspectors' Directory's Home Inspection Checklist at tinyurl.com/inspectionlist

Home inspectors are paid to find things wrong with the house and they will. By crawling under the house and in the attic, they find all kinds of interesting things. It's not uncommon to get a list of repair item(s) five to ten pages long, so don't be surprised. Remember, their interest is the condition of the property, not the outcome of the sale. Inspectors are your opportunity to protect yourself from potential hidden problems and expenses before you take possession of the property.

If the inspector recommends repairs, have them done before the closing or, at the very least, obtain estimates to know what the alterations and repairs will cost after closing. Just because something looks or sounds minor, don't wait until after you own the home to find that the problem is much bigger (and more expensive) than you expected.

Things Not Covered in a Home Inspection Include:

- Asbestos
- Radon Gas
- Lead Paint
- Toxic Mold
- Pest Control

If the inspector recommends repairs, have them done before the closing or, at the very least, obtain estimates.

These items require a specific license to inspect and identify. If you decide to have these items inspected for, your lender or real estate agent will suggest licensed inspectors for you to contact.

Chapter 18

CLOSING COSTS

There are costs, in addition to the purchase price, that you will incur at the time of closing. These *closing costs* are various fees charged by those involved with the transfer of the property from the seller to you, the buyer. Some fees are paid by the seller; some are paid by the buyer. Who pays what is always negotiable. Do not ignore closing costs as part of your total purchase amount.

What the Buyer Typically Pays

- **All fees to do with obtaining the loan**—it's your loan, after all.

- **Appraisal**—you want to confirm your purchase price does not exceed market value.

- **Home inspection**—always have one to know what you are really buying.

- **Pest inspection**—required in most Southern states because, in humid climates, there are many crawly things that eat and destroy homes (termites, powder post beetles, flying ants, etc.).

- **Homeowners insurance**—typically prepaid for one year at closing.

- **Mortgage insurance**—required by the lender if you borrow more than 80 percent of the value of the property.

- **Survey**—often not required, but it does make sure your property boundaries are accurate.

- **Property taxes**—from the day of closing to December 31.

- **Interest**—mortgage interest paid from date of closing to thirty days before first monthly payment is due.

- **Attorney fees**—where applicable.

- **Title insurance**—yours and the lender's.

- **Escrow fees**—if you or the lender choose to escrow any of your taxes or insurance.

- **Loan discount points**—if you paid for a lower interest rate.

- **Fee for recording the documents.**

- **Transfer taxes**—if there are any. Many states charge a tax to transfer property to a new owner. For example, $1 per $1,000 of selling price. Check with your county, not state, to find out your rates.

Do not ignore closing costs as part of your total purchase amount.

Typical Closing Costs and Their Definitions

- **Appraisal Fee.** Your lender will require an appraisal. They want to confirm the value of the property they are lending against. The appraisal fee is paid to an appraiser to obtain an estimate of market value of the property.

- **Attorney Fee.** Attorney fees are paid to the closing attorney or Title Company for closing the transaction.

- **Credit Report.** An evaluation by a credit bureau of the buyer's credit habits.

- **Hazard Insurance.** Insurance that protects a property owner against damage caused by fires, severe storms, earthquakes, or other natural events. Typically, the buyer will be required to pay for a year's worth of premiums at closing, but this will depend on the exact details of the policy.

- **Inspection Fees.** Lenders require a general property inspection before they will lend on a property. There will also be a fee for any inspections you, the buyer, want done including: septic inspection, termite and pest inspections, mold, radon gas, etc.

- **Loan Origination Fee.** A lender's fee to you, the borrower, for establishing a new loan. Conventional loan origination fees range from one to three points. A point is equal to one percent of the loan. For example, on a $100,000 home, a point is $1,000.

- **Mortgage Insurance.** Typically required on conventional loans when you borrow more than 80 percent of the appraised value. The cost may range from a half percent to 1 percent per year and fourteen months premium is often collected at closing. This is coverage for the lender in case you default.

- **Prepaid Interest.** Mortgage interest from the date of closing to thirty days prior to the first regular mortgage payment.

- **Recording Fees.** Charges by the County Recorder to record documents required to clear or transfer title.

- **Survey.** Shows boundaries of a piece of real estate, whether buildings or other improvements are actually located on the property, and that surrounding buildings or improvements do not encroach on the property.

- **Tax and Insurance Escrow.** If the new loan is going to have an escrow account for the payment of taxes and insurance, the lender will require from two to ten months payments to be deposited at the time of closing, depending upon when the next taxes or insurance need to be paid out of the escrow account.

- **Title Examination Fee.** Cost to review the title to the property for liens, mortgages, easements, or defects.

- **Title Insurance.** Covers title defects and certain unrecorded liens that may not be found in the title examination. Cost of title insurance is based on the loan amount or purchase price and is required by most lenders. The cost depends on the amount of the loan for a lender's policy, or the purchase price for an owner's policy. A lender's title insurance policy does not insure owners.

The above fees for processing the loan are typically paid at closing, meaning you must have this money readily available. If rolled into the loan, you will pay these fees plus interest over time.

HUD1 Settlement Statement

Closing costs will be itemized for both you and the seller on a document called a HUD1 Settlement Statement. This form will be filled out by the attorney or title company and will be displayed to both you and the seller at closing to show all fees each of you will pay to purchase, transfer, and record the transfer of property.

Ask that a copy of the HUD1 Settlement Statement be provided to you twenty-four hours before your scheduled closing so that you can confirm all fees you are to pay and the amount you need to bring to closing. This is common practice

Closing costs will be itemized for both you and the seller on a document called a HUD1 Settlement Statement.

OMB Approval No. 2502-0265

A. Settlement Statement (HUD-1)

B. Type of Loan						
1. ☐ FHA 2. ☐ RHS 3. ☐ Conv. Unins.			6. File Number:	7. Loan Number:		8. Mortgage Insurance Case Number:
4. ☐ VA 5. ☐ Conv. Ins.						

C. Note: This form is furnished to give you a statement of actual settlement costs. Amounts paid to and by the settlement agent are shown. Items marked "(p.o.c.)" were paid outside the closing; they are shown here for informational purposes and are not included in the totals.

D. Name & Address of Borrower:	E. Name & Address of Seller:	F. Name & Address of Lender:
G. Property Location:	H. Settlement Agent:	I. Settlement Date:
	Place of Settlement:	

J. Summary of Borrower's Transaction		K. Summary of Seller's Transaction	
100. Gross Amount Due from Borrower		**400. Gross Amount Due to Seller**	
101. Contract sales price		401. Contract sales price	
102. Personal property		402. Personal property	
103. Settlement charges to borrower (line 1400)		403.	
104.		404.	
105.		405.	
Adjustment for items paid by seller in advance		**Adjustment for items paid by seller in advance**	
106. City/town taxes to		406. City/town taxes to	
107. County taxes to		407. County taxes to	
108. Assessments to		408. Assessments to	
109.		409.	
110.		410.	
111.		411.	
112.		412.	
120. Gross Amount Due from Borrower		**420. Gross Amount Due to Seller**	
200. Amount Paid by or in Behalf of Borrower		**500. Reductions In Amount Due to seller**	
201. Deposit or earnest money		501. Excess deposit (see instructions)	
202. Principal amount of new loan(s)		502. Settlement charges to seller (line 1400)	
203. Existing loan(s) taken subject to		503. Existing loan(s) taken subject to	
204.		504. Payoff of first mortgage loan	
205.		505. Payoff of second mortgage loan	
206.		506.	
207.		507.	
208.		508.	
209.		509.	
Adjustments for items unpaid by seller		**Adjustments for items unpaid by seller**	
210. City/town taxes to		510. City/town taxes to	
211. County taxes to		511. County taxes to	
212. Assessments to		512. Assessments to	
213.		513.	
214.		514.	
215.		515.	
216.		516.	
217.		517.	
218.		518.	
219.		519.	
220. Total Paid by/for Borrower		**520. Total Reduction Amount Due Seller**	
300. Cash at Settlement from/to Borrower		**600. Cash at Settlement to/from Seller**	
301. Gross amount due from borrower (line 120)		601. Gross amount due to seller (line 420)	
302. Less amounts paid by/for borrower (line 220)	( )	602. Less reductions in amounts due seller (line 520)	( )
303. Cash ☐ From ☐ To Borrower		**603. Cash** ☐ To ☐ From Seller	

The Public Reporting Burden for this collection of information is estimated at 35 minutes per response for collecting, reviewing, and reporting the data. This agency may not collect this information, and you are not required to complete this form, unless it displays a currently valid OMB control number. No confidentiality is assured; this disclosure is mandatory. This is designed to provide the parties to a RESPA covered transaction with information during the settlement process.

but often does not happen unless there is a specific request for it from the attorney or closing agent.

When you receive the HUD1, typically twenty-four hours before your scheduled closing, examine it to make sure it does not differ significantly from the lender's original good faith estimate. If there are significant discrepancies, have them corrected.

Calculating Your Closing Costs

When calculating your closing costs, always start with your down payment. Lenders typically require 10 percent to 20 percent of the purchase amount as a down payment at closing. This is where the amount you need readily available begins to add up.

Many of these fees are negotiable as is who will pay them, buyer or seller.

Even if paying cash for your home, you will pay closing costs. Fees such as recording fees for the deed, title insurance, and transfer tax still apply. Costs vary from area to area and transaction to transaction, so consult your local real estate agent or attorney to find out which fees you are required to pay. They can also calculate estimated costs you are responsible for based on your purchase price. Again, many of these fees are negotiable as is who will pay them, buyer or seller.

A Final Walk Through

If possible, and it should be, do a final walk through the property the day of closing, before you close. It is important to check the condition of the property one more time and to make sure everything is still there: light fixtures, window treatments, appliances, etc.

Make sure nothing was damaged between the time you and the inspector looked at it and the day of closing. Homes can be damaged during the move-out process and vacant homes may have been vandalized. Confirm what you are buying before you sign on the dotted line.

Chapter 19

THE MOVING PROCESS AND TIPS

Finally, you're moving. Be prepared, be organized and have fun! Last time I moved, we had been in the house for eleven years and our two children had moved out—without all their stuff! We had A LOT to move!

Cleaning Up and Clearing Out

Heads up: when you know you are going to move, join a gym! The amount of physical work you are about to experience cannot be over emphasized. Getting fit will actually help avoid injuries and exhaustion.

So, what's first in the moving process? As soon as you begin to look for your new home, start cleaning out the current one. You can never clean out too soon, too often, or too much. The best Feng Shui advice is GET RID OF THE CLUTTER!

If you are not using something, pass it on. Start the cleaning out process with your shoes and clothes. When the

As soon as you begin to look for your new home, start cleaning out the current one.

clothes are nice enough for someone else to use, but things you no longer wear, pass them on.

Then there are the unnecessary knick-knacks. Pack those up to give away. Cleaning out the closets and drawers is therapeutic. It feels good and increases the energy in your home to get rid of the excess, and to know you are helping someone else who can use what you do not.

Planning a yard sale? I found this great Web site: YardSaleTreasureMap.com. The site allows you to put in your address, the distance you want to drive, and the day you plan to shop. Apparently, the list comes from sales posted on Craigslist. com so, if you plan to sell, be sure your information is posted there so shoppers can find you.

Packing Tips

Start saving newspapers. Ask friends and neighbors to save theirs for you. You can never have too much packing material. Buy bubble wrap for dishes, glasses and breakables. Consider using green packing materials and moving companies, which you can find online.

Grocery stores and liquor stores are great sources for strong boxes (for free!). Cardboardboxes.com is a great resource for buying as well as disposing of cardboard boxes. Most stores crush their boxes after emptying so ask them to save boxes for you. Sometimes they have boxes available, or they may be willing to collect them and tell you when to come back to pick them up.

Old clothes or linens make great packing material.

Do not use paper or plastic bags. Items are not protected, and bags tear and spill. Having everything in boxes makes it so easy to stack and pack in the moving truck.

Cheap paper towels work nicely as packing material since they are clean (no newsprint to transfer), come on a roll so they can be sized appropriately, and can be used for cleaning after you unpack. Old clothes or linens that you plan to donate or throw away also make great packing material.

When packing, use different colored boxes for different rooms. You could also use different colored tape or stickers so you or the movers know which room to take each box in your new home. Clearly mark all boxes. That way, when you get to the new home, you will know where the boxes go, what you want to open first, and what can wait until later or go into storage.

When taping boxes, be sure to use packing tape. It is the only kind that will really hold through the trials of moving. Duct tape does not stick well to cardboard and may break lose. Whatever tape you use, get twice as much as you think you'll need and you'll probably still run out.

Clothes are okay to leave in drawers during transport, but everything else should be taken out and boxed for safety and ease of movement. Take out all valuables, such as jewelry, and anything breakable or heavy.

Always clearly mark the FRAGILE items. Lamps, china, computers, stereos, and DVD players all must be carefully packed and marked for safety. Remember how well they were packed when you bought them?

Wardrobe boxes are a worthwhile investment. Simply take the clothes out of your closets and hang them on the hanging bar in the box. No folding necessary. These boxes save a ton of time and energy. Storage facilities often sell wardrobe boxes and unusually sized boxes for those awkwardly shaped items.

> *When packing, use different colored boxes for different rooms.*

If you are moving appliances, be sure to empty the contents of the refrigerator and freezer. Take everything out of the oven and drawers. All appliances must be empty, drawers and doors secured so they don't fly open during transport.

Scheduling

As soon as you know your moving date, choose a moving company and make a reservation. Especially May through August, available trucks can be hard to find. Ask the moving scheduler what requirements they have for packing your belongings, and don't underestimate how much stuff you have and how much it weighs. The last thing you need is for the movers to show up, only to refuse to load your stuff until they've repacked it, or not load it all because there's not enough room on their truck.

Check and recheck all appointments. When you are packed and ready to go, the movers not showing on time, the cable guy not coming as scheduled, the power company forgetting to send someone to read the meter so they can turn off and/or transfer your electrical, all of these and many other things can really mess up your move. Re-confirm appointments! Make sure the person you talked with really scheduled your appointment. It takes some time, but the mistake you prevent will be well worth it.

> *Things happen. Not everything goes as planned, so expect that when you start out.*

And, Finally

Things happen. Not everything goes as planned, so expect that when you start out. Be well rested and have food throughout the moving day. If possible, have a friend bring dinner over while everyone is unpacking. There is nothing better than sitting down to a wonderful meal when your body is ready to collapse!

There will be repair issues in the new home that you did not expect, so expect them. This is all part of the experience of the new place. You'll want to change things to make the house yours. Give yourself time, do it with love, enjoy every minute of your new adventure and... **Welcome Home!**

Bonus Section

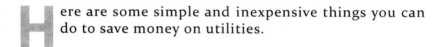

Chapter 20

THIRTY WAYS TO SAVE MONEY ON UTILITIES

Here are some simple and inexpensive things you can do to save money on utilities.

1. **Check it out!** In many areas, cable, satellite, and utility companies compete for customers, so you can save on some utilities by shopping around for the best rates and plans. Be sure to ask about bundles and packages (and consider a switch to basic cable).

2. **Use energy-efficient light bulbs.** This is the big buzz right now. Simply replace incandescent light bulbs with compact fluorescent bulbs. You can now buy round bulbs, not just the corkscrew type, that may look better in some of your fixtures. I found them to be less expensive in multi-packs. There are many types of energy efficient bulbs so shop around for the ones you prefer.

3. **Check your heat and air vents.** Check to see which of your vents are open. Some rooms stay warmer or cooler than others, so adjust the vents to balance the temperature throughout your home. You may find the airflow is better upstairs when you close off some of the downstairs vents. Some rooms may need the vents only partially open. We use one end of our home very little so we closed most of the vents at that end, allowing less energy to heat and cool the rooms we use the most.

4. **Install aerator screens on your faucets.** These little screens distribute water flow so you get more coverage with less water. They increase the pressure of the stream of water as it comes out of the faucet so you don't need to turn the faucet up as high. Screens cut the water flow from three to four gallons per minute to as little as a half-gallon.

5. **Use ceiling fans.** Their rotating direction can be changed depending upon the season. In the summer, you want them to draw the heat up from the floor. In the winter, they should push the heat down from the ceiling.

6. **Put a brick or a sealed jar inside your toilet tank.** This displaces water in the tank so you use less. Careful not to displace too much water or it won't flush properly. I filled a plastic water jug for mine. Buying low-flow toilets can cut water usage down dramatically.

7. **Install low-flow showerheads.** The ones we use create very strong-pressured sprays, and this cheap fix can net significant water savings. Many people fear you give up water pressure, but we didn't find that to be the case. They will save 25 percent to 60 percent of the water you normally use to shower and 50 percent of the energy. Many power companies (including ours) give them away.

8. **Leave the faucet off** when you are brushing your teeth or shaving. Only turn it on when needed.

9. **Wash your clothes in cold water.** This saves 50 percent of the energy you would use for hot water, prevents many set-in stains, and prolongs the life of your clothing. Set your dryer on the moisture sensor if you have one (not the timer) and cut energy use by 15 percent.

10. **Get a programmable thermostat.** And use it—especially if no one is home during the day—to save energy when the house is empty. They're not difficult to install. Some power companies offer a rebate for these thermostats, which can cover their cost. Call to see if your power company participates. Turn the heat down at night when you're sleeping.

11. **Check your air filters.** If your home is heated by forced air, check the filters. A clogged filter considerably decreases the efficiency of your heater. It works harder when it is dirty and you pay for the extra effort it makes to move the air. Air filters are very inexpensive and many should be changed every month.

12. **Service your furnace.** My HVAC guy says they should be serviced every two years for maximum performance.

13. **Use thick curtains.** Covering your windows with heavy curtains can make a huge difference in the warmth or coolness of the room. In the winter, open curtains wide to heat rooms; close curtains at night to keep warm air in. In the summer, get what cool air you can in the evening and early morning; close curtains to keep cool air inside and heat out. Energy saving light-blocker curtain liners can be easily added to your existing window treatments.

14. **Turn down the heat!** Dress warmer at home during the winter and as lightly as possible in the summer. For every degree you lower your home's temperature during the heating season, you subtract 5 percent from your bill.

15. **Stop leaks.** A leaky faucet wastes up to 2,700 gallons per year. Test the toilet for leaks, too. Put a drop of food coloring in the toilet tank. If the color shows up in the bowl, your

tank is leaking and you're wasting up to 200 gallons of water a day.

A leaky faucet wastes up to 2,700 gallons per year.

16. **Use less hot water.** You don't always need hot water to get yourself or your clothes clean. When showering, use warm rather than scalding water. Instead of letting water run until it's warm before washing your hands, go for cold only with good soap.

17. **Weather strip doors and windows.** Stop the airflow. This process is easy, inexpensive and can make a huge difference. In my son's dorm room, we weather stripped around his hall door and were amazed by how it blocked the outside noise!

18. **Insulate your attic access.** Many attic doors or staircases have no insulation on their backside. Yours may also need weather stripping around the sides to block airflow going into and out of the attic.

19. **Insulate your garage.** Especially any walls that are shared with a room in the house. Don't forget to insulate the garage ceiling if you have a room above the garage.

20. **Insulate your water heater.** Buy a wrap for it at a home improvement store. Know how the sides of your coffee mug leaks heat? You get the idea. Consider getting a demand (tankless or instantaneous), heat pump, or solar water heater (although higher energy savings doesn't always mean lower operating costs throughout the year).

21. **Lower the temperature setting on your water heater.** Set the temperature to 120 degrees Fahrenheit. If your heater does not have a temperature gauge, dial down until the water feels hot, not scalding.

22. **Fill up the dishwasher.** With the exception of newer dishwashers that automatically adjust the amount of water and

heat necessary for the load, most of the energy used by dishwashers is to heat a set amount of water so you're using (and paying for) the same energy for a small load as for a full load. If you really want to be economical, let the dishes air dry.

> *Most of the energy used by dishwashers is to heat a set amount of water so you're using (and paying for) the same energy for a small load as for a full load.*

23. **Use switch and outlet energy seals** to stop drafts from coming in through plug outlets. Put your hand by your outlets, especially on exterior walls, to see if you feel cold air coming in. I bought a bag of outlet plug covers at the Dollar Store and put them in all of our outlets that don't have cords in them. You know the kind I mean? The ones you put in when baby proofing your home so children don't stick their fingers in the plug openings? My kids are grown, but I use the covers now to stop any airflow.

24. **Cover fireplace openings.** If not in use, make sure that big hole is covered! Decorative glass doors are easy to find. When those holes are open in the winter, your heat goes right up the chimney!

25. **Check floor heating and air vents.** My inspector pulled ours up to show me the opening left between the floor and the smaller ductwork. I could feel air coming up from under the house so he suggested I use weather stripping or tape to block that airflow before putting the vents back on.

26. **Get a separate water meter** for your exterior hose bibbs and/or irrigation system. In most areas, your sewer bill is tied to your water usage. Why pay more for sewer service in the summer when much of the water isn't going down the

drain? Many water utilities allow you to have dual meters, only one of which gets billed for sewer service (the one that feeds your house).

27. **Plant trees.** Not ones that stay small, but large trees like oaks and maples. Shading your house from direct summer sun will cut way down on your air conditioning bills.

28. **Pull the plug!** This is one of my favorites. Did you know that, of the total energy used to run home electronics, 40 percent is consumed when the appliances are turned off?? When you've turned them off, PULL THE PLUG! Or, you can buy a device to do it for you. Some power strips will stop drawing energy automatically when your electronics are turned off. They pay for themselves in a few months!

> *Of the total energy used to run home electronics, 40 percent is consumed when the appliances are turned off.*

29. **Contact your utility company.** Find out if your utility company offers free energy audits by inspecting your home for energy effectiveness and recommending inexpensive ways to cut energy costs. Ours does. I had to wait several months because they stay so backed up, but they gave me a free energy audit and gifts!

30. **What can you add?** What are you doing (or should you be doing) to save energy?

Epilogue

I have been investing in real estate since 2004. I now coach and train real estate investors who want to learn how to do what we do(check out our website: www.TriadMastermind.com). I also write real estate articles for my blog four to five times per week at www.KarensPerspective.com, and I write books.

What I've found when directing buyers, sellers, and investors to my Web site is that many of you prefer to hold the printed word rather than read a blog. You want to be able to mark it up, make notes in the margins, and tag pages for reference.

For you, I've put together this book taken, in large part, from my blog posts. I've elaborated them in printed form so you have all the information you need to carry with you and reference with ease.

Many thanks to you for your interest, and if you are left with unanswered questions or have a real estate story or success you'd like to share, please contact me on my blog www.KarensPerspective.com, and click on the Contact tab.

I look forward to hearing from you and may you have tremendous real estate success!

About the Author

Karen Rittenhouse is a full-time real estate investor. She's been involved in real estate since 2000, when she purchased her first investment property, and full-time since January 2005. In the past few years, Karen has bought and sold more than 150 single-family homes. She is not a real estate agent. All of the deals with which she's been involved have been her own.

Karen also does local coaching and training, and has found through her travels nationally that many people recognize the value of investing in real estate—some with only their personal homes, others as a way to produce present and future income. Most people simply don't know how to get started, what to do next, or where to get information. That's the purpose of her writing—concise, abundant information.

Before turning to real estate, Karen sold high-end furniture and did interior design. So, as you can see, much of her working career has been involved with creating nurturing home environments. Her goal here is to help people who want to realize the dream of home ownership.

For better understanding, I've listed important terms here alphabetically. They aren't all official definitions; many are friendly explanations as I would explain them in person. For more real estate definitions, check out one of my favorite sites, Investopedia.com.

Absolute Auction—the winning bid purchases the property. There is no minimum bid amount and no need for lender confirmation.

Adjustable Rate Mortgage (ARM)—mortgage where the interest rate paid on the outstanding balance varies over time. The initial interest rate starts low for a period of time and increases periodically, in some cases, every month.

Closing—Finalizing the sale! Time when all documents are signed and recorded. This is the time when the ownership of the property is transferred from seller to buyer.

Comp—in real estate, comp is short for comparable sale. These are sales of similar homes in the same or similar neighborhood as the property being evaluated. By comparing similar characteristics between homes of comparable size, value, and age, a buyer is better able to determine the true property value of the home they want to purchase.

Closing Costs—costs over and above the price of the property, all to do with the transfer of the property. Costs include a variety of things like loan origination fees, discount points, appraisal fees, title searches, title insurance, surveys, taxes, deed-recording fees and credit report charges. These costs are typically paid at the closing.

Counter Offer—an offer made in response to an unacceptable offer. A counter is a new offer and starts the offer process over. A counteroffer is a way to decline a previous offer while allowing negotiations to continue.

Credit Report—evaluation by a credit bureau of the buyer's credit habits.

Credit Score—a numeric expression of your creditworthiness ranging from 350–800.

Debt to income ratio—how much debt you have compared with how much pre-tax income you bring in to cover that debt.

Default—failure to make a payment when due.

Deficiency Judgment—occurs when the lender does not release the borrower from their personal obligation to repay the full amount that was owed before a short sale occurred. In this instance, the borrower remains liable for the full amount of the remaining loan balance even if the property is sold for less.

Discount Points—prepaid interest you can purchase to lower the interest you will be paying monthly. The discount points you buy actually pay the lender their interest today rather than over time. Each discount point generally costs one percent of your loan amount and lowers your interest rate by one-eighth to one one-quarter percent.

Due Diligence—investigation before entering into a contract or agreement with another party.

Earnest Money Deposit—money submitted with purchase and sale agreement to show seller that buyer is serious about purchasing a property. At closing, the deposit is put toward the buyer's down payment.

Equifax—one of the three largest American consumer credit reporting agencies along with Experian and TransUnion. Equifax is the oldest of the three agencies, founded in 1899. It gathers and maintains information on over 400 million credit holders worldwide.

Equity—the difference between what is owed on the mortgage and what the property is worth.

Escrow—monies held by a third party on behalf of lender and borrower. When all agreement conditions are met, the money held in escrow transfers to the appropriate entities. For example, property taxes or mortgage insurance is often "held in escrow" out of every monthly payment until they are due. When the tax or mortgage insurance payment is due, those monies are transferred from your escrow account and sent to pay your tax or mortgage insurance. Most mortgage lenders are not willing to risk that a homeowner will not pay property tax or insurance, so they require these monies to be escrowed.

Experian—a global credit information group like Equifax and Trans Union.

Fair Market Value—the price a given property would sell for.

FHA—Federal Housing Administration—largest insurer of home loans in the world.

FHA Loan—mortgage issued by federally qualified lenders and insured by the Federal Housing Administration (FHA). FHA loans are designed for low to moderate income borrowers who are unable to make a large down payment. FHA loans are popular with first-time buyers because they are able to borrow up to 97 percent of the value of the home. The 3 percent down payment can come from a gift or a grant.

FICO—Fair Isaac Corporation is the company that provides the credit score model to financial institutions.

Fixed Interest Rate—an interest rate that will not change.

Fixed Rate Mortgage—A loan or mortgage that will remain at a constant rate for the entire term of the loan.

Foreclosure—termination of the mortgage rights of the home-owner. Taking possession of a mortgaged property because someone failed to make his or her mortgage payments.

Good Faith Estimate—An estimate provided to the borrower by the lender of the fees associated with obtaining a mortgage loan. The estimate must be provided to the borrower within three days of submitting their loan application.

HELOC—home equity line of credit allowing a homeowner to borrow against the equity in their property.

HOA—Homeowners Association—An organization that assists with maintaining and improving groups of property.

HOA Fees—Money paid monthly by owners of residential property to the Homeowners Association assists with maintaining and improving that property and others in the same group.

Home Warranty—one-year service contract covering repair or replacement of breakdowns of certain home system components and appliances.

Housing Bubble—economic bubble that has rapid increases in property values until they reach unsustainable levels when, at that point, they sharply decline.

HUD-1—form used by closing agent to itemize services and fees imposed on both borrower and seller in a real estate transaction. This form provides each party, at or before closing, with a complete list of incoming and outgoing funds.

Lessee—the person or entity leasing the property as a tenant.

Loan Modification—loan mod—a permanent change in one or more of the terms of a loan.

Loan to Value—LTV—the loan amount compared to the property value. Indicates the amount of equity in the home.

Market Value—the price for which a given property would sell.

Mechanics Lien—Due to non-payment, lien placed against the property by builders, contractors, subcontractors, suppliers of materials or tradesmen who build or repair the structure for any work done or materials used on the property. The lien ensures that they will be paid before anyone else in the event of sale of the property.

MLS—Multiple Listing Service—Where real estate agents publish their property listings.

Mortgage—debt secured by a piece of real estate. Borrower is obligated to pay back the debt with a predetermined number of payments. Also known as a "lien" against the property.

Mortgage Insurance—protects lender or titleholder against losses if the borrower defaults on payments, dies, or is unable to meet the obligations of the mortgage. Mortgage insurance is required for borrowers making a down payment of less than 20 percent.

Mortgagee—lender.

Mortgagor—borrower.

PMI—Private Mortgage Insurance—protects lenders against loss if a borrower defaults. Most lenders require PMI for loans with loan-to-value (LTV) percentages in excess of 80 percent. This means if you buy a house for $100,000 and borrow more than $80,000, the lender will require you to pay PMI.

Points—one percent of the amount of the loan.

Prepayment Penalty—clause in a mortgage stating, if the mortgage is paid off early or refinanced within a certain time period, a penalty will be charged. The penalty is typically a percentage of the mortgage balance or a specific number of months worth of interest.

REO—Real Estate Owned—properties banks own because they have taken them back from borrowers who have defaulted on their mortgage.

Seller Concessions—a specific dollar amount or percentage of the purchase price that a seller agrees to contribute toward closing costs.

Taking Title—transferring legal ownership from the previous owner to the new owner. After transfer, the new owner's name shows on the recorded title to the property.

Tax Credit—dollar for dollar reduction in tax owed. Your gross income is $100,000. You have a $2000 tax credit. You still owe tax on $100,000 but you take $2000 off the total amount you owe.

Tax Deduction—amount you subtract from your gross income to figure out how much of your income is taxable. For example, if your gross income is $100,000 and you have a $2000 tax deduction, your taxable income is now $98,000.

Title—recognition of ownership

Title Insurance—covers the loss of a property due to legal defects. Required on any property with a mortgage. Most title insurance is paid for by the borrower but protects only the lender.

Title Search—examination of public records to confirm property's legal ownership and to discover what claims are filed against the property. Searches check ownership, liens, judgments, loans and property taxes due on the property.

TransUnion—third largest credit bureau in the United States. Offers credit-related information to potential creditors as do Equifax and Experian.

VA Loan—mortgage loan for veterans and their families. The Department of Veterans Affairs does not originate VA loans. They establish rules for those who qualify, dictate terms of the mortgages offered, and insure VA loans against default.

Workout—renegotiation of loan repayment. A new agreement between lender and delinquent borrower.

Internet Resource Links

Calculators

- **Mortgage Calculator**
  mortgageloan.com/calculator/
- **How Much Can You Afford**
  tinyurl.com/homeaffordability
- **Buying vs. Renting Calculator**
  tinyurl.com/shouldirent
- **Should you pay discount points for a lower interest rate**
  mortgageloan.com/calculator/
- **Comparing Length of Mortgage**
  tinyurl.com/mortgageterms

Credit

- FreeCreditReport.com
- AnnualCreditReport.com
- Equifax.com
- Experian.com
- TransUnion.com

Crime Check

- CrimeReports.com
- Crimemapping.com
- Spotcrime.com

Foreclosure Info

- **Foreclosure Laws—State by State**
  tinyurl.com/foreclosurelaws

- **Foreclosure Map—State by State**
  tinyurl.com/foreclosuresbystate

- **Nationwide Foreclosure List**
  foreclosure.com/

Free Sites to List or Find Properties

- **Trulia**
  trulia.com

- **Zillow**
  zillow.com

- **Craigslist**
  craigslist.org

Home Values Comparables

- **Home Values Price Check**
  realestate.com/homepricecheck/

- **Real Estate Values Free Comps**
  realestateabc.com/home-values/

- **Cbyerhomes**
  cyberhomes.com/

- **Eppraisal**
  eppraisal.com/

Maps

- **Bing**
  Bing.com/maps
- **Yahoo**
  maps.yahoo.com
- **Google**
  maps.google.com

Additional

- **Housing Predictor**—forecasts for all 50 states
  housingpredictor.com/
- **Free Look-ups**
  melissadata.com/lookups/
- **National Association of Realtors® website**
  Realtor.org
- **Freddie Mac & Fannie Mae mortgages**
  government-mortgages.com/
- **VA loans**
  homeloans.va.gov
- **Real Estate Definitions**
  Investopedia.com
- **Federal Consumer Protection Agency**
  ftc.gov/
- **Home Inspectors Directory Inspection checklist**
  tinyurl.com/inspectionlist
- **HUD**
  hud.gov
- **Federal Housing Finance Agency**
  fhfa.gov

To Understand the
Selling Process...

Look for Karen's companion books at
KarensPerspective.com, Amazon.com or
wherever fine books are sold!

For more free real estate
information and training,
scan this code or go to
KarenRittenhouseBook.com

CPSIA information can be obtained at www.ICGtesting.com
Printed in the USA
LVOW051521110812

293822LV00008B/147/P